VOLUME 1

A 7 DAY JOURNEY

Insight into the

BIBLICAL

FEASTS

Michael Laws

ISBN: 978-0-9998578-7-8

Library of Congress Control Number: 2019941186

Cover design: Dr. Lavern "Candy" Askew

Published by G Publishing, LLC

Printed in the United States of America.

Table of Contents

Dedication

The first dedication of course, is to YHWH who directed me to study about His Feast Days. He inspired me to write this book to explain His Holy days to all people. Thank you Yah, towdah YHWH.

I also give thanks and dedicate this book to my wife Sandra and two sons, Yusef and Christopher. They are the most important people in my life, and I esteem them highly. Sandra and I have been inseparable now for over 50 years. She inspired me to write this book, even though I never considered myself a writer. This book is dedicated to all of you for tolerating the many years of study day and night while compiling the information for use in this book. Thank you and I love you.

I am also dedicating this book to two very special women in my life. My mother "Eddie Lee Wright" who has now departed this life. This book is for you mom! My mom was a very wise and spiritual woman. Whenever I went to her with a problem, she would always ask, "Mike did you pray about it?" She stood 4'11" tall but to me, she was a giant among women.

My last dedication is to my great aunt "Eddie Lee Stampley" or more affectionately called "Mama Sister." She has also departed this life, but she will never be forgotten. She did not have any children of her own, but she brought all her siblings to Chicago from Vicksburg, Mississippi and raised them. She also took care of my mother and some of my mother's siblings. I never knew my grandmother, however, Mama Sister treated me like she was both my grandmother and mother. She was one of the most influential women in my life.

Acknowledgments

I want to acknowledge my oldest brother Jose, who is now the Patriarch of the family. He too has submitted to his Hebrew heritage. Jose has been not only a brother, but my best friend.

A special thanks go out to W.C. and Lavern "Candy" Askew. Candy is an instructor in the Paleo Hebrew language and the author of several books. She also encouraged me to write and for that I am grateful.

My pastor, District Elder Samuel B. Ware was well versed in Old Testament theology and inspired me on this journey.

Bishop Robert David Young mentored me and provided wisdom on how to Pastor and study. He always said to me, "free of charge."

Stanley and Ellen Bragg are an integral part of my journey because they have encouraged me to write this book and move forward with the ministry.

Introduction

I am writing this book from a Biblical and historical perspective. I intend to reveal many hidden truths concerning the Biblical Feast Days that have been ignored by the modern religious world. For far too long the world have dismissed the instructions that were given to Moses concerning His Feast Days. Most people think the Biblical Feasts are obsolete.

The intent of the book is to enlighten the reader about Elohim's real purpose for sending the Torah and His Feasts to the world. Let the Spirit (Ruach) be your guide as you take this journey with me through the Biblical Feast of YHWH. The objective of this book is to open your understanding of the Bible through His feasts.

I have read many books in my life, but none is more intriguing to me than the Bible. I began reading the Bible well over forty years ago. In the early years it would have been unfathomable to think that reading and deciphering what was in the Bible would become my life's work.

I started my journey seriously reading the Bible as a minister while attending a church in Westland, Michigan. Upon entering the ministry, I was instructed to read the Bible at least once from the beginning to the end. It took me a few years, but I did accomplish that goal several times over.

The Bible is comprised of many stories of characters that lived thousands of years ago. Those stories have captivated the minds of millions of people and quite frankly have shaped much of their lives and behavior. For example, the story of Abraham is an illustration of a person who had enough faith in the YHWH to leave his homeland and venture off to a land that he had never been on the strength that he believed in the promises of the Creator.

The concept of "faith" was the central theme of the Abrahamic story. This compelling story has inspired many people to do things outside of their usual paradigm. The three main religions of Christianity, Judaism, and Islam all claim the personage of Abraham in their literature and history.

The values and principles that encapsulate many of the Bible stories have encouraged, inspired and emboldened millions of people throughout the ages to do things that seemed impossible. People have received healing in their bodies, opened businesses, moved to distant lands to help others and used the principles even to establish nations.

Unfortunately, they have also used this book to plunder, steal and enslave whole nations and people groups. It confuses me to know that many people have used this book to promote their divisive rhetoric. To enhance their fictitious narratives, people have used the book to suggest that others who read it, did not correctly understand it because they don't share the same views. So, they separate themselves and fight against each other.

People are divided into organized denominations that base their foundational principles on concepts that supposedly doesn't exist in the other groups. These differences have caused great schisms within the Body of Messiah. How can we share the same book yet differ so drastically in our understanding? Does the Bible support so many divisions?

The answer to these important questions is because the Bible was translated many times into various languages. The earliest extant of the Bible was the translation from the Hebrew scriptures into the Greek language. They completed this translation around 200-300 BCE. The final rendering was called the Septuagint which comes from the Latin word "Septuaginta" which means seventy. Similarly, the word for the month of September means the number seven. Codex Sinaiticus was handwritten well over 1600 years ago, and the manuscript contains the Christian Bible in Greek. They translated the Septuagint at the request of Ptolemy II Philadelphus who was the Greek king of Egypt from 284 to 243 BCE. He was the son of Ptolemy I Soter, the Macedonian general of Alexander the Greek. The Greeks enjoyed the stories in the Hebrew Bible and wanted a copy for themselves. They say that Ptolemy II had the Hebrew texts translated by 70 or 72 Hebrew scholars (6 from each of the 12 tribes of Israel). Supposedly, they each independently translated identical versions of the entire Hebrew canon.

When I began studying the Bible as a Christian, I did not know that the Bible was not a Greek book nor was it written by the Greeks. Most people give credit to the Greeks for writing the Bible. However, while reading the Bible, it always seemed like I knew the people in the book. Their actions and expressions appeared very familiar to me. I know that the people lived thousands of years ago, but I could relate to them. Reading the Bible was like reading a biographical, historical book about my family.

I also felt that the book was alive. Sometimes while going through a challenge in my life, I would open the book and the scripture that I needed at that time would minister to me as if someone was there talking to me and helping to direct my life. I know that sounds unbelievable, but it is true.

I not only read the Bible for inspiration, but I also studied it for long hours at a time. I have gone through a plethora of emotions while reading the book. Sometimes I found myself laughing or even crying while reading. I guess I can say that the Bible has been like a companion to me. Maybe that is why

I spent most of my life trying to understand the history and the cultures of the people in it.

My wife has excellent spiritual insight. At times, while going through trials in my life, she would encourage me to fast and pray. Our favorite fast was "Daniel fast." This fast consisted of not eating bread, sweets, meat or the drinking of any liquid other than water for twenty-one days. We shut down the television during this period while awaiting a visitation or inspiration from the YHWH. Whatever we needed most, we waited in expectation to receive it. He (YHWH) always demonstrated his faithfulness to us by meeting those needs.

I also believed that He (YHWH) spoke to me. Most of the time I would receive a message from Him that was not audible, but I could hear it in my conscious mind. This may seem a bit mystifying, but I assure you, I am not crazy.

One day, in the early 1990s, while approaching the end of a "Daniel" fast, YHWH spoke to me and said to extend the fast to 40 days. I told my wife, Sandra, what I heard, and she advised me to be obedient. I fasted for 40 days. Near the end of the 40 days, YHWH instructed me to continue for another 40 days. The Most High told me that He would birth something in me if I stayed the course.

I knew that something serious was on the horizon. During these next 40 days, I was directed to read the book of Exodus. While reading chapter 12, I saw something that changed my life. I had read this chapter before and even heard it preached but this time, the meaning of the narrative became clear. Several phrases like "the beginning of months "and words like the new year, lamb and forever took on new meanings. Elohim began to open my understanding of the book of Exodus chapter 12. What stood out most in this chapter was the strong emphasis on the Biblical Feast Day, called

Passover. The scripture indicated that we are to observe the Passover. I couldn't help but think, "what the heck was Passover?" Once I found out what Passover was I also discovered that we were to keep the Feast forever.

I asked my wife to read it just to make sure I was not taking the scripture out of context. She read it and arrived at the same conclusion that the word forever, meant "forever." I began asking questions. If the Bible says to observe the Passover forever, why isn't it happening today?

I figured there must have been a typing error in the Bible, or maybe I did not understand the translation. Every good student of the Bible owned a Strong's Concordance, so I went to the Strong's to see if I could get clarification. The word in Hebrew is "olam" which can mean eternity. Therefore, what I had read was correct, we are to keep Passover throughout all generations to eternity.

To me, this information was life changing. I had been a Christian almost six or seven years and had never experienced Passover in the Christian community. I continued studying and found out that there were six other observations or Feast Days. By now, I became shaken and confused. What else did they "hide" in this book? Why didn't the Christian community observe Biblical Feast Days? The Christians don't seem to have a problem practicing non-Biblical traditions such as (Easter egg hunts, Halloween, and Christmas trees).

Aren't we supposed to base our lives on the principles in The Book? As I learned more about the Feasts Days, I became constrained to teach about them. Little did I know, that the teaching of this information would become my life's work. So, was the Bible translated improperly? Did something happen in the New Testament that eradicated the word "forever?"

I reread the Bible from cover to cover, only to confirm that the "Feast Days" found throughout the Bible still exist and should be observed. The Most High led me to study more Christian history. While doing so, I discovered that some very nefarious things happened during the second century through the fourth century after the death of the Messiah. During that time, the rulers of the world were Romans. They had dominion over most of the known world at that time.

The Roman Empire at its peak
https://www.bing.com/search?q=map+of+the+roman+empire+at+its+pe
ak&form=EDGTCT&qs=SC&cvid=f6a0bfb264874a299f71230cdb8dcf26
&refig=86e121c714a342dbfa9a5d0f

They had the power to pass edicts or laws that would affect people in all the countries under their jurisdiction. Around 321 -325 they eventually passed a series of edicts and bulls which abolished certain Biblical Hebrew practices and observances.

They abolished Sabbath worship and Passover, only to replace them with the pagan holidays and traditions that we see in today's modern Christian community. I also discovered that the Bible underwent a continuous series of translations and transliterations. These translations were significant because the translators were able to insert words in the scriptures that supported their new religious practices and holidays. For instance, the word "Easter" is not in the original Bible translation. However, in many Bibles today, you can find the word in the book of Acts. Why was it inserted in some translations, and for what purpose?

Wasn't the Septuagint a good enough translation? Why did they have to change it? The Septuagint translation remained as the standard for nations up until the 4th and 5th century CE. The drawback of this translation was that it was written only in Greek and needed to be read and taught in other languages.

In the year 382 AD, Pope Damasus I commissioned Jerome to revise the Vetus Latina Gospels (Old Latin Bible) which was then heavily in use by the Roman Church. Jerome whose name was Eusebius Hieronymus began writing his translation in the 4th century and completed it in the 5th century AD.

They refer to his work as the Latin Vulgate. The purpose of this translation was so the Catholics of that era could understand it. The Latin Vulgate became the official Bible used by the Catholic Church. Suffice it to say that the Bible went through a complete "makeover." Because the Romans remained the most influential religious body, most people and nations conformed to the traditions, practices, and norms of the Catholic church.

Later, there began a movement to reform the Church to the standards of the times. This reformation movement began with certain groups breaking away from the Catholic Church and forming what we call denominations. Therefore, the Catholic universal church is considered the mother of all the various denominations. A denomination is defined as a branch of a religion.

Leslie J. Hoppe, a Franciscan friar, has been Professor of Old Testament Studies at Catholic Theological Union in Chicago since 1981. https://www.christianitytoday.com/.../jerome.html

St. Jerome seems to have used as the basis of his revision a Greek MS closely akin to the *Codex Sinaiticus. That he revised the remaining books of the NT is unlikely." (The

Oxford Dictionary of the Christian Church, Vulgate, 2005 AD) The Bible also went through more translations. The next group of translations came about during the periods between 1400 and 1800 AD around the time of the Transatlantic Slave trade. Before that period, an English priest and professor at the University of Oxford who was a dissident to the Roman Catholic Church wrote his translation in the modern vernacular of that time. He completed his translation directly from the Vulgate into Middle English. This new translation was completed in the year 1382 AD and is now known as Wycliffe's Bible. By the time that they wrote the King James Version translation, the Book had been translated or transliterated almost fifty times from the original. During this period, many of the translators injected their ideology into their writings.

For example, around A.D. 140-150 - Marcion of Sinope's of Rome established a New Testament canon, and he promoted a two God system of belief which still exist today. He ultimately rejected the Hebrew/Eber scriptures now called the Old Testament. His beliefs are still being taught today. _https://www.biblegateway.com/resources/encyclopedia-of-the-bible/_.

Many people do not believe that there were so many translations of the Bible prior to the King James version. What becomes clear after extensive research is that the authority, ownership, and commentary of the Bible still rest with the Catholic Church and the Pope.

Most of the translations that spun off after 500 A.D. were from protestors or reformers. Even though they broke away from the Catholic Church, they still used the Catholic dogma including Constantine's Apostolic doctrine as the foundation of their belief system. This division is the reason why there is so much confusion! It is apparent that there is only one original and if you want to understand the original you have to reference the Hebrew language. It is imperative that you try to understand the language, culture, and intent of the original writings.

One of the keys to understanding the Bible is knowing that the original scriptures were not written in Greek, Latin or the English language to Christians. The original was translated into Greek. There is still debate over which translation was more accurate, the Vulgate or the hand written Codex Sinaiticus.

The original Bible was written in the Hebrew language, by Hebrews, about Hebrews. It is a very spiritual Hebrew history book. When you read it using Greek lenses, Roman lenses or English lenses, the true meaning of the Hebrew messages become concealed.

Greek thought emphasizes abstract ideas, but abstract concepts do not entirely convey an original Hebraic point of view. The Hebrew thought is clear and concise, usually based upon a specific action. For example, when we hear the Hebrew word *shalom*, we usually translate this word to mean peace or absence of war or strife. However, the Hebrew word shalom has a very different meaning. The verb form of the root word is *shalam* and used in the context of making restitution. When a person has caused another to become deficient in some way, such as a loss of livestock, it is the responsibility of the person who created the deficiency to restore what has been taken, lost or stolen. For example, "the Hebrew/Eber verb *shalam* means to make whole or complete." The noun *shalom* has the more literal meaning of being in a state of wholeness or being without deficiency. The Biblical phrase "shalu shalom yerushalayim" (pray for the peace of Jerusalem) is not speaking about an absence of war (though that is part of it), but that Jerusalem, and by extension

all of Israel, be complete and whole and goes far beyond the idea of "peace."
(Ancient Hebrew Dictionary, Jeff A. Benner, published 2009, Virtualbookworm.com Publishing Inc. pp. 151)

The Bible and the religion of the people of the Book, has undergone many transformations whether through translations or the invention of customs and practices that relate to it.

The Bible and the religion of the people of the Book never changed. Each of the translations went through many transformations. Sometimes the translators inserted some of their own customs and practices.

I challenge you to take a second look at the so-called Old Testament scriptures. In them, the Creator gave us a set of instructions to help us to live peaceably among one another.

The jazz artist Leon Thomas sang the lyrics to the legendary, Pharaoh Sanders' composition, "The Creator Has A Master Plan". They apparently believed in the existence of a Creator and not some theory called "evolution." They knew that Elohim had the power to create everything in this world within a well-orchestrated plan.

The Creator did not create us to wander despairingly in the earth, He sent us a set of instructions to help us execute this master plan. Those instructions were called Torah but, later, through the process of translations, they were re-labeled as "law." The good thing is, YHWH never abolished them! If we would just adhere to His instructions, the world would become a better place to live.

As you go on this "7-day journey" with me, please listen with both your mind and your heart. We pray that Elohim will open your understanding of His Biblical Feast Days.

Chapter One: Why the Biblical Feast Days?

People today think that we are much more intelligent than the people that wrote the Bible. We believe that we have a more developed science and mathematical understanding of time and space. We are now able to calculate time down to the atomic-second. Aren't we smarter than our predecessors? Why is it important to the observe the Feast Days written in the Bible rather than keep our traditional holy days?

When looking at our Biblical past, we are like cave dwellers. We certainly are educated with some of the best education that money can buy. However, biblically a great many people are illiterate as it relates to the Bible.

Many of us who read the English version of the Bible think that we have a good understanding of it. Remember, the Bible was translated or transliterated almost fifty times before the "1611 King James Version" was printed.

Let me stop to clarify two terms that we have been using, "translate and transliterate." The word translate means to turn something written or spoken, from one language into another: to change into another form; transform or convert. The word transliterate means to replace letters, words into corresponding characters of another alphabet or language; *The American College Dictionary pp1287, Random House New York L.W. Singer Company. Syracuse, NY copyright 1963, 1964, 1965, 1966, By Random House, Inc.*

The Hebrew language has words that cannot be translated or transliterated along linguistic lines. When they translated many of the words or phrases, unknowingly they changed the context of the sentences. This caused some verses to take on a different meaning than what the writer intended. For example, let's review the first sentence in the Bible. The first sentence in the Bible says much more than the transliterations reveal. For instance, in English, the sentence reads, "In the beginning, God created the heavens and the earth." (Gen. 1:1)

In the Hebrew language, it reads בְּרֵאשִׁית בָּרָא אֱלֹהִים אֵת הַשָּׁמַיִם וְאֵת הָאָרֶץ:

Each Hebrew letter in the aleph-bet has a name, a number, a meaning, and a sound. The first seven words in the Hebrew Bible reads, "B'reshit bara Elohim at hashamayim vaat haeretz.

(B'reshit) The first word "reshit" means beginning. The letter "bet or B" in front of reshit means "in."
(Bara) The second word "bara" means to create.
(Elohim) The third word in the sentence is "Elohim." This word means "God or Powers."
(at) The fourth word in the first sentence of our Bible is "at אֵת." This word "at" represents the entirety of the Hebrew aleph-bet. The first letter of the aleph-bet is "Aleph." The last letter of the aleph-bet is "Taw or tav." There is no English equivalent for this word.
(hashamayim) The fifth word in the sentence is hashamayim which means the heavens
(va'at) The sixth word in the sentence is va-at. The term "va" in front of a word means "and."
(haeretz) The seventh and final word in the sentence is haeretz which mean the earth.

If we look at just the first four words in our Bible in the Hebrew/Eber language, it reads the following; "In the beginning, God created the Hebrew language from the aleph to the tav." The word "at" (aleph tav) represent the beginning and the ending of the Hebrew aleph-bet. However, based upon the writings of Yahshua (Jesus), the letters "at "(aleph tav) represent Him.

We know that Yahshua (Jesus) spoke Hebrew and Aramaic to his followers. He referred to himself as being the aleph (alpha) and tav (omega). The question becomes "why was the scripture translated using Greek terms (alpha and omega) rather than the Hebrew (aleph and tav)?"

Revelation 1:8 I am Alpha and Omega, the beginning and the ending, saith the Lord, which is, and which was, and which is to come, the Almighty.

The word Alpha is the first letter of the Greek alphabet and omega is the last letter. It seems rather baffling how the translation of the Hebrew word, "at" (aleph – tav) could end up with a Greek expression, "alpha and omega." Most scholars know that the Greek alphabet is a copy of the Hebrew alphabet with only a few minor changes. Notice the following example;

(aleph, bet, gimmel, dalet -vs- alpha, beta, gamma delta)

The writer John was a Hebrew and the words that Yahshua spoke was derived from his Hebrew manuscript. Were there political and theological motivations behind this change from "Hebrew aleph to Greek alpha?" We don't know the answers to this disturbing question, but we are aware that Yahshua would have used the Hebrew terms, aleph and tav. (at)

The first four words of the Bible therefore can read, In the Beginning, created Elohim, "at" or aleph and tav which became the Hebrew language. This sentence can also infer that the aleph and tav were the Elohim who created. If

Yahshua was the "at" (aleph-tav), then the "aleph tav" was the Elohim.

In the original ancient pictorial Paleo Hebrew, the letter aleph is shaped like an ox head or mature sheep's head with the horns. This pictograph of the ox head means strong leader. The Hebrew letter tav is in the shape of an "x" or cross which means covenant or sign. When you put the two letters together, they denote a strong covenant. If you look even closer, it also purports that the alef/tav represents a person who would seal a strong covenant.

If you don't believe that example, then let's examine the balance of the sentence. We already gave you the meaning of the fifth word, "hashamayim" as heavens and the seventh word, "haeretz" as earth.

The sixth word in that same sentence is truly fascinating. The sixth word, "va at" is comprised of the Hebrew letters "vav, alef, and tav." You already know that the letters alef and tav (at) are the letters at the beginning and end of the Hebrew Alphabet and it means a strong covenant.

The writer place the letter "vav" before the "at" 𐤀+ in the sixth word of that sentence. The ancient pictorial Hebrew letter "vav" is shaped like a nail or tent peg. 𐤅 It means nail, hook or connection. When you put all three letters together of the word "v at" and apply the meaning of each letter, the sixth word should now read, "the nail connected the strong one to the covenant cross." What an awesome picture in the first sentence of our Bible! + 𐤀 𐤅

I know that right about now you are about to fall out of your chair if you are reading this with your spirit and your heart. Notice that the sixth word "v at" sit <u>between</u> the fifth word "hashamayim or heavens" and the seventh word "ha Eretz or earth." Now, if you put the fifth, sixth and seventh words together, it would read slowly in English,

"The nail connected the strong one to the covenant cross between the heavens and the earth."

This is an amazing revelation. Does that remind you of anyone? Please keep in mind, you cannot see this revelation when you read the sentence in English, Latin or Greek!

The native tongue of Yahshua was Hebrew. If you read Rev. 1:8, using a Hebrew mindset, it is clear that Yahshua would have said, "I am the Aleph and the Tav,"meaning "I am the strong one on the covenant cross who was there in the beginning."

Rev. 1:8 I am Alpha and Omega, the beginning and the ending, saith the Lord, which is, and which was, and which is to come, the Almighty.

Now we understand what the writer of John 1:1 meant when he wrote that Elohim (God) was the word. He was most likely referring to the Aleph / Tav. $\triangleright$+ (strong covenant cross)

John 1:1. In the beginning, was the Word, the Word was with Elohim (God), and the Word was Elohim (God).

Once you begin reading the book of Genesis, B'reshyth using your Hebraic mindset, it becomes clear that the first thing that the Creator designed was His Word or His Aleph-Bet.
There are other examples demonstrating the ancient Paleo Hebrew letters;

The first letter of the Hebrew alphabet is aleph. Written in modern Hebrew it looks like, (א). The meaning of this first letter is that which is strong. In the ancient Paleo Hebrew alphabet, it was drawn like the head of an ox or ram. ﾆ The ancient Hebrew letter (tav) looked like a cross. ✝ The letter tav means a mark, sign, and "covenant." Also, the letter tav, represented a person's signature. Many people today, continue to substitute their signatures with an "X."

These two Hebrew letters, "aleph and tav," represent the entire Hebrew aleph-bet and can also be interpreted to mean, Elohim's (God's) signature. Therefore, if we look at the aleph tav from a pictorial Paleo Hebrew context, it tells us that the "aleph tav" את is a strong sign, representing the Creator's signature. ﾆ✝

As you can see, the Paleo Hebrew language provides a much clearer insight into the scriptures than what we gather by reading the Bible from a Greek or English perspective. Our knowledge of the Hebrew scriptures is quite limited if we only use an English translation. In comparison, the Hebrew language gives us more depth and meaning.

The first sentence of the Bible explains the entire plan of salvation for humanity. There is so much more to uncover in the first verse of the Bible, however, we won't cover it at this time!

The first word of the Bible is "B'reshit."   This word is comprised of the letters beyt, resh, aleph, shin, yod and tav.

The first letter beyt means tent or house. The Paleo Hebrew letter is shaped like an aerial view of an ancient tent. ᗰ Therefore, the first letter in the Bible reference a house.

The second Hebrew letter in the Bible is the letter resh. This letter means head, summit or first. The Paleo Hebrew letter is shaped like the head of a person. ℜ The first two letters of the Bible reference the head of the house. When you put the first letter beyt with the second letter resh, it spells "bar" which means son. ℜ ש So far, the first two letters of the Hebrew Bible purports that the "head of the house is the son."

The third letter which begins the Hebrew Bible is "aleph." The letter, aleph, means a strong leader. The ancient Hebrew pictorial letter is shaped like an ox head or mature sheep head. ⅄ In ancient times they used to yoke an older stronger ox with a younger less mature one. The stronger ox would show the younger how to bear the burden in the field. Now, the first three letters of the Hebrew Bible suggest that "the strong one that bears the burden in the field is the son who is the head of the house."

The fourth and fifth letters, shin and yod, spell the word "se" which means lamb. ﾑ ⌒ The fourth, fifth and sixth letters in the Hebrew Bible spell the word, "shyth" which means thorns. ✝ ﾑ ⌒ The sixth letter in the Hebrew Bible is the letter "tav." The letter tav means covenant and is shaped like a cross.

When all the first six letters of the Hebrew Bible are combined, they reveal that "the strong son who is the head of the house was the lamb who bore the burdens for the weak ones and was crowned with thorns on a covenant cross." What an amazing revelation that was found in the first six letters of the Hebrew Bible. This information can not be found in the English translation. The plan of salvation for mankind is found in the Hebrew Bible within the first six Hebrew letters.

If you deny the existence of the Son, then the book is of no value to you except as a good novel. The entire Bible is about the revelation of Yahshua ha Mshiach.

Chapter Two: Signs in the Heavens

And God said, let there be lights in the firmament of the heaven to divide the day from the night; and let them be for signs, and seasons, and for days, and years: (Gen. 1:14)

Genesis 1:14 deals specifically with the luminaries in the sky that give light to the earth. We also use them to provide our measurement of time.

The 14th verse of the Book of Genesis (B'reshit), declares that the Most High created the heavenly bodies, sun, moon, and stars for signs and seasons. The scripture references in Gen. 1 became the basis of our initial understanding of time. We use this chapter to help us understand how to calculate the days, weeks, months and years. We are also able to use them to quantify the spatial relationship of light and darkness to the earth.

When you read Gen. 1:14, on the surface, it also says that the sun, moon, and stars are unquestionably used for the calculation of the seasons of the year. The scripture does mention the English word, seasons. We, therefore, surmise that we must use the heavenly system let us know when the seasons change and how to prepare for such changes. Most of our natural behavior is associated with the changes that occur with each season. Our clothing and habits are all linked to the seasons and time. A wise man said that there is a time for everything under the sun. "A time to reap and a time to plant."

In contrast to the English language, when you read the Bible from a Hebrew perspective, many reflective, hidden messages are revealed. Always remember, the original Bible was written in the Hebrew language, not the Greek, Latin or English.

Gen. 1:14 And Elohim (God) said, let there be lights in the firmament of the heaven to divide the day from the night; and let them be for signs, and seasons, and for days, and years:

Gen. 1:14 וַיֹּאמֶר אֱלֹהִים יְהִי מְאֹרֹת בִּרְקִיעַ הַשָּׁמַיִם⬚הַבְדִּ֜⬚ בֵּין הַיּוֹם וּבֵין הַלַּ֜֜ה וְהָיוּ⬚אֹתֹת נ⬚מוֹעֲדִים ⬚יָמִים וְשָׁנִים:

This verse provides us a discourse regarding the things that happened on the fourth day of creation. In English, it says that Elohim created the heavenly elements sun, moon and stars to be as signs and seasons for us.

What does that mean to you? Does it infer that we are to use the lights to help us determine when to plant our food and when not to? Of course, it does! We have learned through trial and error that planting certain seeds during prescribed periods, increase the life cycle of that seed. Does the Bible say that the astrological charts will dictate our personality? Should we look to the heavens for daily guidance? No!!!

The Hebrew language is linguistically beautiful. One Hebrew word can have up to 8-10 English meanings. The Hebrew language can compare to a diamond. When you hold the diamond in the light, it may reflect numerous colors, but if you turn it, the reflection differs. We have already witnessed veiled messages in the first sentence of the Bible. Many other verses have meanings that are not distinctive in English. Could the 14th verse of Genesis be constructed the same? Let's examine this verse little closer to see what we can discover.

Genesis 1:14 was written regarding the 4th day of creation. We know that on the first day of the creation, Elohim spoke "light" into existence. On the fourth day, He made manifest the sun, moon, and stars to give light to the earth. What was the fundamental purpose for the luminaries?

When most people read Gen. 1:14, they read the unembellished English translation. There is no reason to question the intent of this verse. On the surface it appears explicit and unambiguous.

Gen. 1:14 And Elohim (God) said, let there be lights in the firmament of the heaven to divide the day from the night; and let them be for signs, and seasons, and days, and years:

Based on what we have witnessed so far, could there also be a hidden message in Genesis 1:14? We will observe two words in that verse that may have deeper meanings than what we might have initially thought. In the English translation, the words that we will examine, are signs and seasons. The Hebrew word for "sign" is "owth." אֹת. The writer wrote the word "otot," for the plural, signs. The singular Hebrew word "owth" is a fascinating word.

It has the same letters as discussed in the previous, chapter involving, Genesis 1:1. The sixth Hebrew word in the first sentence, "v at" has the letters (vav, alef, and tav). Both words (owth and vaat) possess the same Hebrew letters. In the Hebrew word (owth), the letter vav is placed <u>between</u> the Aleph and the Tav instead of being located <u>before</u> the alef and tav asin the case of "vaat." The Hebrew letters are read from right to left. (✝ Ⲩ 𝒷) "aleph, vav and tav."

In the Hebrew aleph-bet, the letter (vav) looks like a nail or peg used to connect the walls of a tent. The word (vav) in the Bible means a "hook or nail." When used in a sentence, the word (vav) is a conjunction, and is translated in English, to the word "and." This letter is used to connect two prevailing thoughts. If you place this letter (vav) between the Aleph and the tav, it could read that, "the strong one is connected by nail to the covenant cross." We now grasp a similar picture as the one revealed in Genesis 1:1.

It should be clear that the message in the letters (alef, vav and tav), allude to Yahshua (Jesus) who became, "the strong one that was nailed to the covenant cross." After this great event occurred at Calvary, it caused such a powerful reaction from heaven, that the sun refused to give light and the earth became darkened.

Luke 23:44, 45 And it was about the sixth hour, and there was a darkness over all the earth until the ninth hour. Moreover, the sun was darkened, and the veil of the temple was rent in the midst.

Notice, the writer Joel, mentions the luminaries as <u>signs</u> from heaven. Let's survey more scriptures which reference the heavenly bodies as signs from heaven.

Joel 2:30-32 And I will <u>shew wonders in the heavens</u> and in the earth, blood, and fire, and pillars of smoke. The sun shall be turned into darkness, and the moon into blood, before the great and the terrible day of the LORD come. And it shall come to pass, that whosoever shall call on the name of the LORD shall be delivered: for in mount Zion and in Jerusalem shall be deliverance, as the LORD hath said, and in the remnant whom the LORD shall call.

Luke 21:25 And great earthquakes shall be in divers' places, and famines, and pestilences; and fearful sights and great <u>signs shall there be from heaven</u>.

Joshua 10:13-14 And the sun stood still, and the moon stayed until the people had avenged themselves upon their enemies. Is not this written in the book of Jasher? So, the sun stood still in the midst of heaven and hasted not to go down about a whole day. And there was no day like that before it or after it, that the LORD hearkened unto the voice of a man: for the LORD fought for Israel.

2 Kings 20:9 And Isaiah said, <u>this sign</u> shalt thou have of the LORD, that the LORD will do the thing that he hath spoken: shall the shadow go forward ten degrees, or go back ten degrees?

The Bible clearly shows that "signs" are related to the heavens. They are more than lights that help us calculate the seasons. They act as witnesses to the greatest show on earth, the cross at Calvary and the future regathering of Elohim's bride.

Did you know that there are 7 Biblical Feasts and on three of them, there is always a full moon in the sky? (Passover, Unleavened Bread, The Feast of Tabernacles) When the Feast of Trumpets occur, there is a new moon in the sky as well. We must, therefore, become more observant of the changes that occur in the sky because they are signs and messages that reveal the timing of His Feast Days.

Chapter Three: Why are Seasons Significant?

The other word used in Genesis 1:14 is the word "seasons". Most of us believe that the word "seasons" refers to the different seasons of the year, such as spring, summer, fall, and winter. Our school teachers taught us since we were children, that the word season refers to times of the year like spring and summer.

We looked forward to the change of the seasons from winter to spring because it meant that the school year was almost over, and summer was near. We could hardly wait for the summer to come. It was so exciting to feel the change in the weather! We could now spend more time outside playing and doing the things we love to do.

We need to remember that the Bible was not written in the English language. The Hebrew word that designates the seasons of the year is the word "onah." This word "onah" does, describe seasonal changes such as spring, summer, fall or winter. Surprisingly, however, the Hebrew word "onah" was not used in the Genesis 1:14 verse.

The Hebrew word used in Gen. 1:14 was the word (moed or moedim) "מֹעֲדִים." The translators chose as their translation, the English word, "seasons" to describe the Hebrew word moed. The translation using the English word seasons, can be a bit misleading even though one of the meanings of the word moed denote seasons, also.

However, a more concise meaning of the word moed signify an appointed time, feast or festival. There is no question that the translation using the English word seasons fit the verse in Gen. 1:14. However, the Hebrew word "moed" is better understood meaning feasts and appointed times. Let's examine the use of moed in Leviticus 23:2, where the word means feasts or appointed times.

Leviticus 23:2 Speak unto the children of Israel, and say unto them, Concerning the feasts "מֽוֹעֲדֵי" moedi of the LORD, which ye shall proclaim to be holy convocations, even these are my feasts.

In the above scripture, the translator chose not to use the translation of the English word seasons, but he used the word, feasts. In this verse, the translator did not use the word "seasons" because the Hebrew word *moed* has a more contextually concise meaning as a feast, festival and appointed times. You ask, what is the difference? Why did the translator choose to use the translation "seasons" in Gen. 1:14 and a different translation using the word "feasts" in Lev. 23:2 for the same word? Does it make a difference?

Unlike the Greek language, the words in the Hebrew language are exact and concise. When we go back to Gen. 1:14 and apply the proper translation for the term "moedim" of feasts, festivals, appointed times and rehearsals, we get a different understanding. By applying the Hebrew word "moedim" in this verse, it becomes clear that the Most High was not only going to use the luminaries as a sign from heaven, but He was also going to use them as a signal to assist humanity, during His appointed meetings.

Elohim declared on the 4th day of His creation, that he set appointed meeting times. This declaration was made, even before he made man. The Most High made Adam on the sixth day! By the time Adam was created, his meeting and appointment times, were already scheduled. There are four of the "Feast Days" that occur on either a full moon or a new moon on the Hebrew solar/lunar calendar.

What does the word time mean?

According to the dictionary, it is the system of those relations which any event has to any other as past, present, or future. It is also an indefinite continuous duration regarded as that in which events succeed one another. Time is considered intervals which follow the correct rhythm or tempo.

(The American College Dictionary, Random House New York, L.W. Singer Company, pp.1268, Copyright, 1963, 1964,1965,1966, by Random House, Inc.)

The scriptures are clear concerning how to measure time. Numerically, time is measured using either blocks of "60" or "12." Sixty seconds become one minute, and sixty minutes become one hour. Twenty-four hours become one day, divided into two 12 hours sections. Thirty days become one month, and 12 months make one year. In the following scriptures the Most High mentions that the 24-hour day begins in the evening and goes from evening to evening. However, He divided the day into two twelve-hour periods. One twelve-hour period is from the evening to the morning and from the morning to the evening which will total twenty-four hours.

Gen. 1:5 And Elohim (God) called the light Day, and the darkness he called Night. And the evening and the morning were the first day.

John 11:9 Jesus answered, Are there not twelve hours in the day? If any man walks in the day, he stumbleth not, because he seeth the light of this world.

Dan. 7:25 And he shall speak great words against the most High and shall wear out the saints of the most High and think to change times and laws: and they shall be given into his hand until a time and times and the dividing of time.

Today's Time:

One of the reasons why the people today don't understand the Bible is because time has been changed. We operate today on Roman time. We have am and pm which is from 12:00 am to 12:00 pm. This system of time is in direct opposition to Biblical time. We will explore this phenomena in the coming chapters.

Chapter Four: Pagan Times /New Year

Is our concept of time aligned to that of the Bible or has it changed? Are our present religious communities marching to the beat of a different drummer? When is the Biblical new year? Is it in January immediately following Christmas?

One of the most challenging parts of our lives is how we deal with time. Most of us become joyful when the time comes for our birthday, or we become gloomy on the anniversary of a loved one's death or burial. We get stressed out because we are running late for work or it is time for an important meeting. We base our relationship with time on our activities and experiences. Even though time is an abstract concept, we have learned that it can be measured and used to benefit us in our daily living.

The new year that we currently observe is celebrated on January 1 each year. We have customs that have been passed down from generation to generation. In the Christian community, it is customary that immediately after the count down on New Years' Eve, we celebrate by prayer and praise. Some people shoot guns as a tradition. This custom, however, has been the source of controversy lately because sometimes the bullets go through the roofs or enter houses and injure or kill people and damage property.

Another custom that I have seen practiced is to prepare black-eyed peas on New Year's Day and a male must be the first one to come through the door of your house. I grew up observing some of these customs, and my siblings keep them even until now. I am sure you have some traditions as well.

The Biblical new year is not the same as the secular New Year.

We base our customs and practices upon times that were changed by the Catholic Church. When did the change take place and why?

Let's begin by examining the ancient Roman Calendar which should provide some insight as to when and why they changed the time. In the year 753 BC at the time of the first king of Rome (Romulus), there was no formal written calendar. The Romans divided the year into ten months. This Roman calendar also had weeks that consisted of nine days. Therefore, during the time of Romulus, the Romans only had ten months.

CALENDAR BY ROMULUS

MARTIUS - 31 DAYS
APRILIS - 30 DAYS
MAIUS - 31 DAYS
IUNIUS - 30 DAYS
QUINTILIS - 31 DAYS
SEXTILIS - 30 DAYS
SEPTEMBER - 30 DAYS
OCTOBER - 31 DAYS
NOVEMBER - 30 DAYS
DECEMBER - 30 DAYS

https://www.timeanddate.com/calendar/roman-calendar.html

They named four of the calendar months after Roman Gods. The month Martius (March) received its name after the "God of War." Aphrilis (April) got its name after the goddess "Aphrodite." They named Maias (may) after the goddess of spring. An Iunius (Juno or June) was the Protector of Marriage.

The other six months were Roman numbers. (Quintiles "five," Sextilis "six," Septem "seven," Octom "eight," Novem "nine," and Decem "ten." The modern (Gregorian) calendar kept the names of the old early Roman calendar months. In the year 45 BC the Julian Calendar was presented by Julius Caesar. It was assembled in consultation with eh Alexandrian astronomer Sosigenes and was probably designed to approximate the Egyptian tropical solar year.

(By the year 46 BC, Rome had conquered Egypt and took over the hegemony that was once the conquering right of Alexander the Greek.) Once the conquerors arrived in Egypt and North Africa, they seized the ancient knowledge of that part of the world and began to call it their own.

This is evident in the fact that after Pompilius the Etruscan inserted the two additional months to replicate the Egyptian calendar, they never changed the names of the months, with the exception that when Julius Caesar instituted his reforms, he named the 5th month which was called "Quintilus meaning five" after himself (July). Later, Augustus Caesar named the month following July," Sextilus meaning six" after himself as well.

https://www.sabbathtruth.com/free-resources/article-library/id/916/...
www.calendar-origins.com/calendar-name-origins.html

The early Roman Calendar began its year in the month of March. Their year was so far off that the agricultural seasons of the year, would not line up with the months. When Julius Caesar became Emperor, people were complaining so much that he commissioned an Egyptian/Greek Alexandrian astrologer named Sosigenes to correct this problem. In the year 46BCE, Sosigenes added two months. They inserted two months, January and February.

- *The Editors of Encyclopedia Britannica,* ^ *Dialetis, Dimitris (2007). "Sosigenes of Alexandria." In Hockey, Thomas; et al. Biographical dictionary of astronomers. Vol. II, M-Z. Springer. p. 1074.*

January received its name from one of their Gods "Janus" who was considered the God of beginnings and transitions. They depicted this god as a man with two faces looking forward and backward at the same time. It was also considered the protector of gates, archways, and doors.

After over a week of celebration of the pagan holiday of Saturnalia, they would pray to their favorite God Janus, to wipe away their misdeeds from the previous year and provide good fortune for the coming year. We see vestiges of this in the celebration of Christmas and New Year.

Chapter Five: Christmas Magic

Christmas is considered a magical time of the year by many people. It is also considered the birth period of Yahushua. During this time, you see people stringing lights outside and inside their homes. People bring evergreen trees inside their homes and churches with the hope that a man dressed in a red and white suit would visit (preferably) down the chimney bearing gifts to put under the tree for the whole family. It is a very festive time of the year.

People in the business world increase their stock in anticipation of their highest sales volume during this time. They have parties for the employees that include drinking and dancing and other merriment. Mistletoes dangled everywhere. The custom was if you are found standing under it, you must kiss the person next to you.

Despite how much fun and festive this holiday season may be to you, Christmas is of pagan origin. Many people from various countries brought with them their pagan customs and traditions. We practice many of these traditions today in our homes, churches, and schools. The Bible even speaks about some of these traditions. For example, the Christmas tree chronicled in the book of Jeremiah.

It *Jer. 44:25* is *associated with Asherah or Ashtaroth. This goddess is also known as the Queen of Heaven and consort of Baal.*

The tree was associated with the Queen of Heaven. One of the Christmas traditions is to purchase a live tree that had recently cut down. The tree was brought into the house and screwed or nailed to a base so it would remain secure. Most people adorn the tree with bulbs and other ornaments in gold and silver colors. Afterward, they stand back and admire how beautiful it is. Our traditions are almost identical to the sins that our forefathers were admonished against by the Prophets.

Jer. 10:1 Hear ye the word which the LORD speaketh unto you, O house of Israel: 2. Thus saith the LORD, learn not the way of the heathen, and be not dismayed at the signs of heaven; for the heathen are dismayed at them. 3. For the customs of the people are vain: for one cutteth a tree out of the forest, the work of the hands of the workman, with the axe. 4. They deck it with silver and with gold; they fasten it with nails and with hammers, that it moves not.

In many early American colonies, they outlawed the Christmas tree and many other traditions of Christmas. When the Irish Catholics arrived, they brought with them their blended beliefs in Druidism and Roman Catholicism. The Druids believed in luck, fairies, Celtic magic, elves, leprechauns, and Christmas trees.

During the late 1800s, a pharmacist invented a beverage by the name of Coca-Cola (sweetened cocaine). This beverage became very popular and still exists today. One of Coca-Cola's advertising and marketing managers adapted the Dutch/Irish idea of Santa Claus as an advertising campaign. He aligned the campaign with a 2 ft — tall elf called Santa Claus which had its roots in Druid magic. The original Santa wore green and had a long white beard. This creature had the power to grant wishes, watch you while you could not see him and because of his height, could come down the chimney into your home.

Coca-Cola's marketing manager, Mr. Sundblom changed Santa to a chubby full-sized man with the colors of the coke product, red and white. His message in the campaign was to hang a stocking near the furnace with the hopes that the elf/Santa would leave presents under the tree. Just like his predecessor, he also had magical powers.

The poisonous mistletoe is also a druid custom. The mistletoe is considered probably the most magical, mysterious, and sacred plants in Druid folklore. The tradition of kissing under mistletoe began in 1520 when William Irving wrote: "A young man should pluck a berry each time he kisses a young girl beneath the hanging plant, and once the berries were gone the romantic power of the plant faded." Therefore, many gentlemen sought mistletoe cuttings with an abundance of berries to hang in their homes. In modern society, we still carry on this tradition even though it is purely pagan.

Finally, it is imperative that we discuss the parties and merriment that occurs during this time. There was an ancient Roman celebration called Saturnalia which celebrated the Roman god Saturn. (We derive the name Saturday from this god.) The celebration ran for seven days that occurred on Dec. 17 and ended at the birth of the new sun (winter solstice). Everyone engaged in extreme merriment which included drunkenness and lewdness. It is interesting that the birth of the ancient Nimrod supposedly occurred in this same period.

After they finished their week of drunkenness, a week later they celebrated the New Year by praying to Janus. This god of past and present, gates and doors were supposed to bless them with a bountiful year and open new doors for them. I know by now you are saying; it sounds quite similar to the behavior of the people of today.

February is noted for many celebrations and having only 28 days. One of the main traditions was the celebration called **Lupercalia**. This was a very ancient, possibly pre-Roman pastoral annual festival,[2] observed in the city of Rome on February 15. The celebration was to avert evil spirits and purify the city; releasing health and fertility. Lupercalia was also called "dies Februatus," purified (literally "februated day") after the instruments of purification called "februa," which give the month of February (*Februarius*) its name.

At the Lupercal altar, a male goat (or goats) and a dog were sacrificed by one or another of the *Luperci*, under the supervision of the Flamen dialis, Jupiter's chief priest.[11] An offering of salted meal cakes, prepared by the Vestal Virgins.[12] After the blood sacrifice, two *Luperci* approached the altar. Their foreheads were anointed with blood from the sacrificial knife, then wiped clean with wool soaked in milk, after which they were expected to smile and/or laugh.

The sacrificial feast followed, after which the Luperci cut thongs (known as *februa*) from the flayed skin of the victim, and ran with these, naked or near-naked, along with the old Palatine boundary, in an anticlockwise direction around the hill. In Plutarch's description of the Lupercalia, written during the early Empire,

Many of the noble youths and the magistrates run up and down through the city naked, for sport and laughter striking those they meet with shaggy thongs. Many women of rank also purposely get in their way, and like children at school present their hands to be hit. They believed that the pregnant would thus be aided in delivery and the barren to pregnancy.

https://www.history.com/news/why-do-we-kiss-under-the-mistletoe

In modern times, we don't necessarily run through the streets naked in an anticlockwise direction celebrating the fertility holiday of Lupercalia. However, we have still managed to slip in the celebration of another pagan holiday called, Valentine's Day.

The origin of Valentine's Day is still partially aligned to Lupercalia. The Roman Catholic church, in an attempt to stop the bloody celebration of Lupercalia, chose the 14th of February as a day to honor one of the three martyred patron Saints, named Valentine.

This celebration occurs during the same time period as Lupercalia. It is said to be a mixture of Lupercalia and a time to celebrate love and lovers. They use the Cupid as their image which is a young boy with wings and a bow and arrow.

Cupid is the most famous of Valentine symbols and everybody knows that boy armed with bow and arrows, and piercing hearts. He is known as a mischievous, winged child armed with bow and arrows. The arrows signify desires and emotions of love, and Cupid aims those arrows at Gods and Humans, causing them to fall deeply in love.
https://www.theholidayspot.com/valentine/cupid.htm#2FkWkylLf wAJFOWm.99

Most of the modern holidays that we celebrate are extremely pagan. Christians and merchants alike, have embraced these celebrations. To abolish them would cause an uproar within the society not to mention have a negative affect on the economy. Did you know that you were celebrating falling in love with one of the pagan Roman gods? Just a thought!

The History of the Modern Calendar:
The modern calendar history is shrouded in paganism and deceit. Many people think that the ancient calendar was the science of the Greeks or the Romans. To the contrary, they can only take credit for the gross paganism that they applied

to it. They pilfered their calendar from the Sumerians and Egyptians then they modified it and gave it their Greek and Roman names.

The Egyptians and the people of Kush were masters in the field of architecture, building, and astronomy. They built many structures that are considered wonders of the world. For example, the Egyptians built the Pyramid of Giza in 4000 BCE. Sitting in front of the Pyramid is the Sphinx which is human hybrid consisting of an Egyptian bust (head) with the body of a lion. The Sphinx suggested that the Egyptian king was more than a man. He ruled the animal and human kingdoms with superior intelligence. The hieroglyphic meaning of the Pyramid square represents space, constellation, and cosmos.

The Kings Chamber of this pyramid measures 365.25 Pyramid inches which are the same as the number of solar days within a year. The Queen's chamber measures from the floor to the ceiling 364 pyramid inches which are the number of days in a lunar year.

Exhibit 1 Pyramid of Giza/Khufhu built 4000 BCE

They designed the base of the Pyramid to be observed from above. Notice these great structures as viewed from above.

The Pyramid's base was made up of granite, and the measurement is 365.25 Pyramid Cubic. ns.

Moses knew of the exactness of the 365.25 solar years. When researching the 365.25 solar years, I found that the Greeks attempted to take credit by suggesting this knowledge originated from Sosigenes of Alexandria who was an astronomer living in Egypt, but, THIS KNOWLEDGE PRE-DATED GREECE BY ALMOST 4000 YEARS.
www.biblenumbersforlife.com
http://en.wikipedia.org/wiki/File:Giza_pyramid_complex_(map).S VG

The circumference measures 3652.50 Pyramid cubic. The meaning of this Pyramid encircled is the measurement of a land or city in the constellation of Orion. We are not sure of the original name of the zodiac. It probably carried a different name at the time of the building of the pyramid. The name of the constellation is now Orion, a hunter in Greek mythology. The Greeks are late comers that pilfered this knowledge from the Egyptians.

Chapter Six: What is Biblical Time?

The Most High indicated in Exodus chapter 12 that He wanted the beginning of the year to start at a specific time on a particular month. How did Moses know when a month began and when it ended? It is apparent that he possessed knowledge of the use of solar and lunar time. He knew how to measure the days, months and years.

Ex. 12:2 This month shall be unto you the beginning of months: it shall be the first month of the year to you.

The Bible even uses the word time in its writings. The very first time that the transliterated word 'time" was used in the Bible was *"Gen.4:3 And in the process of time it came to pass, that Cain brought of the fruit of the ground an offering unto the LORD"*. The word "time" in the Hebrew language was Strong's 3117 "yomim" which means days or time. (יָמִים).

This word is an unused root meaning to be hot, a day, or warm hours, whether sunrise to sunset, a space of time defined by an associated term, age, day, evening, now, required, seasons.

The second word used to relate to time was found in *Gen. 18:10 And he said, I will certainly return unto thee according to the time of life; and, lo, Sarah thy wife shall have a son. So, Sarah heard it in the tent door, which was behind him.*

Strong's 6256 ayth (עת) now, when, after, continually, from 5710 adah, to advance, pass on or continue.

This word (✝ ◉) is spelled using *the Hebrew letters "ayin" and "Tav" and is also spelled using the "ayin" and the "dalet."* (Ʋ ◉) In the Paleo Hebrew, the meaning of "ayin" is insight and consciousness. In the pictoral Hebrew it is shaped like and eye. The meaning of "tav" is the covenant or cross. This word (✝ 👁) can mean "inight into the covenant cross."

Using that same pattern, the Hebrew word for Dalet in the Hebrew word "ad" means door, portal or entrance. The Hebrew word for time, (Ⅴ👁 ayin dalet), can be considered to also mean, the conscious insight into the event of the bloody door. Most people will not enter a door unless they know what is on the other side. The "ayin" and the "dalet" are dependent upon each other. Therefore, the Feast days are set periods in time that provide an insight into a coming event. They act as His rehearsals for an eternal event that occurred at the covenant cross.

If I invited you to my wedding, the first thing you want to know is when and where is the event going to take place. Before you start planning, you need to know how much time you have for preparation. You mark your calendar to make sure you remember the date. Next, you make a conscious effort to arrange your life schedule to attend the event.

The event "planner" controls the elements associated with the event. This includes the place, the attire and the type of gifts to be given at the party, depending on the culture and tradition. If the attendee (you) agree to attend, the planner adds his name and starts to prepare for his arrival. The attendee selects the proper attire and gifts that he will bring.

If the attendee says to the event planner, I know that your event is on the 12th day of the month, but I will be there on the 13th. What should be the expectations of the attendee? If he shows up a day late, he should not expect to be in the "now" of the event. He should also be aware that the ceremony that he had come to witness had already taken place and no other attendees would be there. Also, if he does not show up on the 12th, he will have missed the event altogether.

The Most High is a date setter. YHWH has invited humanity (Hebrews) to meet Him at specific times on particular days. We have arrogantly chosen not to come at all.

Exodus 12:1 And the LORD spake unto Moses and Aaron in the land of Egypt, saying, this month shall be unto you the beginning of months: it shall be the first month of the year to you.

In the scripture mentioned above, the Most High set specific dates to meet the people of Israel. The first month of the year means "new year." The Hebrew term for the new year is "Rosh HaShanah." Rosh in Hebrew means head, a person in authority or leader. The Hebrew term "ha" simply means "the." The Hebrew term "shanah" means a year which is a period of 365 lunar/solar days. (Rosh Ha Shanah)

This statement of 365 lunar/solar days on the surface may seem redundant, but during the time of Moses, the Hebrews were well versed in solar and lunar days.

The term, day or Yom, in Strong's Concordance, refers to evening and morning or night and day. The period from one midnight to the next in our modern time is called a solar day. A lunar day is from evening to evening.

Gen. 1:5 And God called the light Day, and the darkness he called Night. So, the evening and the morning were the first day.

Many people in today's modern world debate the efficacy of the lunar day. We live in a society that adheres to the Gregorian calendar. This calendar uses solar day schedule. It is therefore difficult to comprehend a book which operates under a lunar/solar day. There are many people today that challenge the evening to evening time period for a 24-hour day.

Yahshua clarified this issue in the scripture;

"John 11:9,10 Jesus answered, Are there not <u>twelve hours</u> in the <u>day</u>? If any man walks in the day, he stumbleth not, because he seeth the light of this world. 10. However, if a man walks in the night, he stumbleth, because there is no light in him."

Gen. 1:5 And God called the light Day, and the darkness he called Night. And the <u>evening</u> and the <u>morning</u> were the first day.

Yahshua states that there are equally 12 hours of daylight and 12 hours of the night for those people that did not understand Gen. 1:5. We must, therefore, conclude that from evening to morning and from morning to evening made up a completed 24-hour day. Once we understand how time is measured Biblically, it will become easier to understand the Feast Days of Yahweh.

Gen. 1:14 And Elohim (God) said, let there be lights in the firmament of the heaven to divide the day from the night; and let them be for <u>signs</u>, and <u>seasons</u>, and for days, and years:

The Bible has many insights and answers to our questions. Elohim shows us signs and wonders in the earth, but we ignore them daily. Signs are everywhere that you turn, in the water, the trees, the vegetation but more importantly, in the heavens. We all have the same book or manual, but we ignore what we read, or we learn without understanding.

When I was young, my mom used to send me to the grocery store with a list of items to get. This list was specific with the brand names of the things along with the cost of each piece to the penny. She was such a good shopper that she memorized the prices of the items that she wanted most. She also totaled out the list with what she thought the final cost would be which in most cases was either exact or within pennies.

Her final instructions were to bring back the correct change. She had already calculated the transaction. I was quite young between 8-10 years old when she began to trust me to send me to the grocery store. I learned quickly to count my change and compare it to the change amount that she calculated on the list. If the totals were off, I needed to let her know of price changes that caused this discrepancy.

My mother knew the end from the beginning so to speak. The Most High is even more exact, and it is certain, He truly knows the end of all things from the beginning.

Isaiah 46:9,10 Remember the former things of old: for I am Elohim (God), and there is none else; I am (God), and there is none like me, Declaring the end from the beginning, and from ancient times the things that are not yet done, saying, my counsel shall stand, and I will do all my good pleasure.

Therefore, if you want to know what the ending is going to be like, then you need to start at the beginning. YHWH declared from ancient times the things that are not yet done. He declared the end of "time" from the beginning of time.

The Bible begins with the Book of Genesis (B'reshit) and ends with the Book of Revelation. Genesis is considered in modern times, the "Old Testament," and Revelation is in the "New Testament." Most people believe today that the things in the "Old Testament" have been done away. However, most scholars know that there are over 300 references in the Book of Revelation to the "Old Testament." If the so-called "Old

Testament" is obsolete and irrelevant, why does the New Testament refer to it at all?

Most Preachers quote the adage, "Old Testament concealed, and New Testament revealed." One of my favorite pastors, Bishop Robert David Young, used to quote the following scripture all the time,

"Proverbs25:2 It is the glory of God to conceal a thing: but the honor of kings is to search out a matter."

If the word "moed" in Hebrew refers to an appointed time, why does the Christian community have such a difficult time acknowledging the Biblical Feast Days? One of the answers may lie in the fact that our modern world is on the Gregorian calendar.

Before we had this current calendar, we were governed by the Julian calendar. Before the Julian calendar, there was the Ancient Roman calendar. Prior to the ancient Roman calendar, the Egyptian and Sumerian calendars were pretty much the standard to follow.

Chapter Seven: The Biblical Calendar vs Pagan Calendar

What happened to the Biblical calendar and does it still exist? The dilemma that the modern Christian community face is how to determine when the "Feast Days" and appointed times will occur.

We are commanded to meet Him at certain times throughout the year, but how do we ascertain when? If we are to meet Him, we must learn what and when the Biblical meeting times are. Elohim's (God) has a rhythm. How do we get in sync with him? We need to understand His timing and rhythm. We have already shown that the Gregorian calendar is steeped with holidays that honor pagan gods. We will now show how the original Biblical times were changed.

The Biblical Day:
What does a Biblical Day consist of? The original Hebrews observed their day from evening to evening. (Lev. 23:42) It was divided into morning, noon and evening. The day (light) consisted of twelve hours from sunrise to sunset. (Matt. 20:1,2) The night was divided into three watches, from sunset to midnight, from midnight to cock crow and from cock crow to sunrise.

The Biblical Month:
The months were lunar (relating to the moon). Gen. 1:14.... and God said, let there be lights in the firmament of the heaven to divide the day from the night, and let them be for signs, and seasons, and for days, and years:

The terms moon and month are closely related terms. The word "menses" is Latin for moon. There is also a connection between the woman's monthly "menstrual" cycle and the waxing and waning of the moon.

The Hebrew term for the month is "Chodesh," and the term for the new moon is "Rosh Chodesh." The Hebrew word "Rosh" means head, beginning or summit. The word Chodesh means month or 30-day period when measured. Each new month started another 30-day cycle.

Did you know that Yahshua (Jesus) is revealed in the cycles of the moon? Let's take a close look at the moon phases.

Psalms 19:1 [[To the chief Musician, A Psalm of David.]] The heavens declare the glory of God; and the firmament sheweth his handywork.

In the Biblical calendar, the new moon begins with a sliver of light and waxes until the 14th and 15th day. On those two days, the moon becomes full. After the 15th day of the month, the moon starts to wane until the 27th day when it disappears for 2 ½ days and finally reappears or resurrects on the third day. Does that sound familiar?

The moon plays an important role in Elohim's master plan because the feasts of Passover, Unleavened Bread and Tabernacles occur on the 14th and 15th day of the Biblical month.

The Biblical Week:
The primary meeting that Elohim set up was a weekly meeting called Shabbat. This important meeting was to occur weekly on the seventh day cycle. This day is currently called Saturday in honor of the Roman god Saturn. YHWH declared Shabbat (Saturday) a day of rest and a permanent meeting day for each weekly cycle. In case you have forgotten, Sunday is the 1st day

of the week. Sabbath has not been changed since the beginning of time. Our weekly cycle still consists of seven days.

About 1400 years ago Sabbath worship of the Creator was officially moved to Sunday by the Roman Emperor Constantine who called himself, the Pontifex Maximus, "God's chief high priest on earth." Constantine chose to change the devotion of the Most High to the same day that he worshipped his sun god, Mithrias.

The Catholic Church, along with other pagan cultures introduced Sunday worship, Christmas, New Year, Easter, Halloween, and Valentinus's Day into modern customs and practices. These holidays have become standard within the Christian ideology no matter whether a person attends church regularly or not.

Many people today, misunderstand and misinterpret the Bible. In order to get a proper understanding of the Book, you need to read it from a Hebrew language perspective. The Bible was written in the Hebrew language using Hebrew idioms, customs, and practices.

The term "seasons" (*moedim*) in the Bible refer to appointed meeting times, festivals and days. No one can change the Most High's set times. The Most High is Sovereign. He wants to meet us on His terms and at His set times and not when we choose to meet Him.

Now all these things happened unto them for ensamples: and they are written for our admonition, upon whom the ends of the world are come. (1Cor. 10:11)

The most misunderstood day of the week is the seventh day called Shabbat. Each day of the week is essential to the Most

High, but great emphasis was placed on Sabbath as His weekly meeting time. In the Hebrew language, this day is called the Shabbat. It is the seventh day of the week. He called every day by a number, but He gave the seventh day a name. The verb, Shabbat means to cease, rest, or intermission.

The Sabbath/Shabbat has been ignored and even shunned in the modern religious world. People work, play and run errands on Sabbath/Shabbat. In modern America, Sabbath is not considered a day off. In the retail sector, which is in the business of buying and selling, Sabbath is the busiest day of the week. There is nothing wrong with buying and selling, however, Biblically, it is strictly prohibited on Shabbat.

If Yah were to question us as to why we did not honor the Sabbath/Shabbat, we could not give a definitive answer. We are programmed by the world, to conduct our business on Shabbat. We work hard from Monday through Friday. Because of that, it seems natural to do the things on Shabbat (Saturday) that we didn't do during the week. Therefore, our society disregards the Sabbath and treats it like a normal workday.

The late great Lou Rawls sang a song with the lyrics, "the eagle flies on Friday but Saturday I go out to play." That song still rings true today as most people use Shabbat as the day of play.

In many parts of the world, but especially in America, the Sabbath/Shabbat has become just another common day of the week. In stark contrast, the first day of the week called "Sunday" has become recognized as a sacred day. As children, we were told to prepare our clothing on Saturday night so that we could attend church on Sunday. Our parents did not want us to spend too much time getting ready for church. In some households, the meal was prepared the evening before to prevent cooking on Sunday.

Sunday had a particular spiritual significance, probably because that was the day set aside for worship of Elohim (God). In some churches, depending on the denomination, the people stay in church all-day Sunday.

Even though Sunday is the most segregated day of the week, we still use that day as the day we give homage to Elohim (God). The Christian community may argue and contend with each other regarding the name of God or whether He is three in one or two in one, but they still manage to all meet up on Sunday.

How is it that we all worship at times that is utterly contrary to the Good Book that we all read, honor and follow?
One of the reasons for our confusion concerning which day is Sabbath/Shabbat is because of the change in the names of the days of the week.

Instead of the word Sabbath/Shabbat, we use the pagan word Saturday. Since the word "Saturday" has been handed down from one generation to the next, we never seemed to question its meaning or origin.

While growing up, Saturday did not seem holy or sacred. If you look up the meaning of the word Saturday, you will find that the name was dedicated to a pagan god called Saturn. Since everyone in our orbit used Saturday (Sabbath/Shabbat) to play, it became a natural habit to work, play, shop and commit evil on that day.

In the lyrics of the song that Lou Rawls sang, "the eagle flies on Friday and Saturday I go out to play" he also refrains, "Sunday I go to church, and I kneel down and pray." It is evident that I am a serious fan of Lou Rawls's music. Going to church on Sunday was and still is the most natural thing to do. We reverence Sunday as a day of worship even in our songs.

The enemy is cunning! He devised a very evil dastardly plan to get us to completely ignore the one day (Shabbat) that should be given over to the Most High. What a genius plan!

Daniel 7:25 And he shall speak great words against the most High and shall wear out the saints of the most High and think to <u>change times and laws</u>: and they shall be given into his hand until a time and times and the dividing of time.

The Catholic Church ordered the whole world to worship on Sunday. We have been more obedient to the Catholic Church than we have been to YHWH. Sunday worship is now considered sacred. We never question why we have certain traditions; we just do them unconsciously.

Sunday worship is now the standard throughout the world. We further cement the concept of Sunday worship by training generation after generation in Sunday school. Each child becomes a new prospective customer for Sunday worship.

When I grew up, there was complete reverence to the day called Sunday. On Sunday morning I saw people dressed in their most beautiful clothing, some walking and some riding to the church of their choice.

Each church may have had different traditions, liturgy, and customs but the one thing they had in common was that they all met on a <u>wrong</u> day, "Sunday." If Sunday is the wrong day, then when is the right day? How can I prove which day is right or wrong? The Bible clearly illustrate what days are the prescribed days for worship. The weekly day of worship and prayer outlined in the Bible is Sabbath/Shabbat.

Genesis 2:3 And God blessed the seventh day and sanctified it: because that in it he had rested from all his work which God created and made.

In the scripture, Genesis 2:3 the writer mentions the name Shabbat as the seventh day of creation. It also mentioned that Elohim blessed the Sabbath. If the Most High Elohim blessed that day, no one has the authority to abolish it. "Shabbat" is a Hebrew word for which there is no equivalent in most languages. The transliteration of the word "Shabbat" to the English language is Sabbath. The meaning of the word derives from a verb meaning to rest, a loss of time, cease or desist from labor.

Shabbat was a creation of the Most High himself! The Elohim created all things in a period of six days, but on the seventh day, He rested from His actions. To be fair, modern society still recognizes the seven-day cycle. However, they do not acknowledge the Sabbath day as a day of rest.

Gen. 2:2 And on the seventh day God ended his work which he had made, and he rested on the seventh day from all his work which he had made.

Immediately after He rested, He _sanctified_ the day. The Hebrew word for sanctify is the word qadesh. *Strong's Concordance 6942 list _qadesh_ as being a primitive root meaning to be, make, pronounce, or observe as clean, (ceremonially or morally): appoint, bid, consecrate, dedicate, defile, hallow, (be, keep) holy, prepare, proclaim, purity, wholly and set apart.*

The New Strong's Exhaustive Concordance of the Bible, pp 102 copyright 1990 by Thomas Nelson Publishers.

This definition indicates that from the beginning of time, the Most High set a specific day of the weekly cycle as a day to observe as clean or pure. It is on this day that we have an appointment to meet with Him. Shabbat was sanctified as holy or set apart. The Most High commanded Moses in;

Exodus 20:4 "Remember the sabbath day, to keep it holy."

YHWH knew there would come a time that people would defile the day of Shabbat. He, therefore, commanded us to "remember the Sabbath day (Zakar Yom Shabbat) and keep (Shamar, guard) it holy (qadesh) set apart. He knew that we would eventually ignore Shabbat once the Hebrews came into lands that did not honor this great day. So, He commanded us to guard it the Sabbath and set it apart from the other days of the week.

The act of remembering is a process. Once you lose the habit of worship on the Shabbat, you must consciously remind yourself that this day Shabbat must be honored. Hebrews honor the Shabbat from sixth day evening "Friday" (6:00) to seventh day evening "Saturday" (6:00). When sixth day evening (6:00) comes, you must cease from all work. This requires a deliberate effort. The Shabbat is the sign of our Covenant relationship with the Most High.

The western culture gave each day of our modern week a pagan name. The first day of the week is named Sunday. Haven't you often wondered where the name "Sunday" derived?

From prehistoric times to the close of the fifth century of the Christian era, the worship of the sun was dominant in pagan cultures. Legend has it that the Biblical Nimrod died, and his body was cut into 14 pieces. His wife Semiramis found his phallus and it is said that from it, she miraculously conceived

Tammuz. She declared that Tammuz was reborn as Nimrod and the people were directed to worship the sun in honor of Nimrod. This is quite simar to the story of Osiris, Isis and Horus.

The following sun goddess names represent Semiramis;

Ishtar -   Babylon
Isis   -   Egypt
Aphrodite - Greek
Ashtaroth - Canaan, Syria
Venus -   Rome
Frigg -   Nordic, wife of Odin
Colombia - Female virgin goddess America

The sun gods to name a few were, Baal, Osiris, Ra, Helios, Apollo, Zeus, Ogmios, and Mithras. The metal, gold as dedicated to the symbols of alchemy or sorcery is associated with the sun god and Sun-day.

They never tried to hide the name. To this day, we pronounce the name of the day as Sun-day. We say it with profound conviction in our conversations, "I can't wait until Sun-day to go to my church." Your church is not the issue. Why do we give homage to the Sun god without questioning the origin of what we do or say?

My generation has been programmed to believe in the sanctity of Sun-day as if it has some spiritual or mystical power. Grant you, all of the days no matter what you call them belong to Elohim. Please stop and think about what you are doing when you name one of His days after a pagan god.

The Days of the Week

In the year 321, Constantine the Great ruled that the first day of the week or "the venerable, most respected day of the sun' should be a day of rest. The sun's old association with the first day is responsible for the fact that the Lord's Day of Christianity bears the pagan name of Sunday.
Interactive Technologies, LLC 1998, The Origins of The Days of the Week
http://www.eliki.com/ancient/myth/daily/sunday/content.htm.

Figure 1

Image of the Sun god Mithras. (Sunday)

Monday is the second day of the week, the day of the moon goddess, Selene, Luna, and Mani. Derived from Lunae Dies, the day of the moon, the name reflects the ancient observance of holy days dedicated to moon goddess or planet. The metal silver dedicated to the moon is associated with Monday.
Interactive Technologies, LLC 1998, The Origins of the Days of the Week
http://www.eliki.com/ancient/myth/daily/monday/content.htm.

Figure 2

Image of Selene goddess of the moon. (Monday or Moon-day)

Tuesday is the third day of the week. In the Roman calendar, the corresponding day was dies Martis, the day of Mars, associated with Ares. Tiw's day is derived from Tyr or Tir, the god of honorable war, the wrestler and the son of Odin and, or Woden, the Norse (Norwegian or Scandinavians) god of war and Frigga, the earth mother. His emblem is the sword, and in olden days the people paid him great homage. Tuesday was named in his honor. The metal iron, dedicated to Mars and interpreted as his spear and shield, is an attribute of Tuesday. *Interactive Technologies, LLC 1998, The Origins of the Days of the Week*
http://www.eliki.com/ancient/myth/daily/tuesday/content.htm

Figure 3

Tyr the Norse god of War. (Tuesday or Tyr's-day)

Wednesday is the fourth day of the week, corresponds to the Roman Dies Mercurii. The name derives from the Scandinavian, Woden (Odin), the chief god of Norse mythology, who was often called the All-Father. Quicksilver, liquid mercury that contains amounts of the platinum group metals, has been interpreted as the caduceus of the Greek Hermes (Mercury in Roman myth) and is, therefore, an attribute of Wednesday. *Interactive Technologies, LLC 1998, The Origins of the Days of the Week*
http://www.eliki.com/ancient/myth/daily/wednesday/content.htm

Figure 4

Statue of Odin, Wodin the Norse god called "All-Father."
(Wednesday or Wodin's-day)

Thursday is the fifth day of the week. It derives its name from the Middle English Thoresday, or Thursday, corresponding to the Roman dies Jovis. Thor, the god of strength and thunder, defender and help in the war, son of Odin, is the counterpart of Jupiter or Jove. Thor is one of the twelve great gods of northern mythology. He is the only god who cannot cross from earth to heaven upon the rainbow, for he is so heavy and powerful that the gods fear it will break under his weight. It was said that whenever Thor threw his hammer, the noise of thunder is heard through the heavens. Thursday was sacred to Thor. The metal tin is associated with the thunderbolt of Jupiter (Zeus in Greek myth) and is an attribute of Thursday. *Interactive Technologies, LLC 1998, The Origins of the Days of the Week* *http://www.eliki.com/ancient/myth/daily/thursday/content.htm*

Figure 5

Thor the Norse god of strength and thunder. (Thursday or Thor's-day)

Friday is the sixth day of the week. The name is derived from the Germanic Frigga, the name of the Norse god Odin's wife. Frigga is considered to be the mother of all, and the goddess who presides over marriage. The name means loving or beloved. The corresponding Latin name is Dies Veneris, a day dedicated to Venus, the goddess of love. The metal copper, dedicated to Venus, is associated with Friday. *Interactive Technologies, LLC 1998, The Origins of the Days of the Week* <u>*http://www.eliki.com/ancient/myth/daily/friday/content.htm*</u>

Figure 6

Frigg the god Odin's wife, goddess of love. (Friday or Frigg's-day)

Saturday is the seventh day of the week, corresponding to the Roman dies Saturni, or day of Saturn, the Roman god of agriculture. Saturday is also represented by Loki, the Norse god of trick and chaos. The metal lead is associated with eh scythe of Saturn and is, therefore, an attribute of Saturday. *https://www.bing.com/search?q=saturday+named+after+saturn&form=E DGEAR&qs=SC&cvid=fe9fa1bb*

Figure 7

Roman god Saturn devouring his son. (Saturday or Saturn's-day)

As we have observed, a pagan god or goddess depict each day of the week in western culture. Without knowing, we have been calling these names and summoning their attributes.

It is shameful to know that the Shabbat (Sabbath) is now given a name that represent Loki, the Norse god of tricks and chaos. Perhaps, that name is fits, because it is a fact that we are all confused and have been tricked, hood winked and bamboozled. Shabbat was supposed to be set aside as a meeting day with the creator. However, we have trampled upon it, completely ignored it and called upon some god of tricks on His day. *Sabbath* is a time to draw closer to the Most High through the study of His word, enjoy family and friends and enjoy a meal of praise unto the Creator.

Mark 2:27-28 And He (Yahshua) said to them, the Sabbath was made for man, and not man for the Sabbath. Therefore, the Son of Man is also Lord of the Sabbath.

The Christian community believes, without support, that Paul the writer of the Epistles, rejected the Shabbat. That is not true! Paul continued to worship Elohim and observe the Shabbat.

Acts 13:14 But when they departed from Perga, they came to Antioch in Pisidia, and went into the synagogue on the sabbath day, and sat down. 15. And after the reading of the law and the prophets, the rulers of the synagogue sent unto them, saying, Ye men and brethren, if ye have any word of exhortation for the people, say on.

Did Yahshua keep/observe the Sabbath? Yes. Did Paul observe the Sabbath? Yes!!! As we indicated prior, the Shabbat has changed in the year 321 AD by the Roman Emperor Constantine. There is no Biblical evidence to support a change from the seventh day of the week to the first day as a day of rest.

When Emperor Constantine changed the day, all of the subjects in every province of the empire eventually adopted this change.

No matter what country that you visit, Sunday is a worship day. The influence of the Emperor has far-reaching implications even until now.

Today, since the invention of the mobile phone, knowledge is right at a person' fingertips. All you have to do is google the word Sunday, and the verification of what I'm saying will pop up. Why do Christians argue about the validity of Shabbat vs Sunday? It is a moot point and can be proven simply by the touch of your finger on your phone.

All Bible believers are commanded to keep the Sabbath, and it is not optional. However, I am beginning to believe that most people don't believe in the book as much as they do traditions, and the socialization they get from their churches. I am saying this in love. "Come out from among them and be ye separate (set apart) says Yah."

In Mathew 5, Yahshua said that *"I did not come to destroy the Torah (law)or the prophets, but to fulfill."* Yahshua did not say that He ended the Torah/law. He meant that His living would provide a better understanding of the Torah. Most people stop at the statement concerning fulfilling the law, but they should continue reading.Notice what it says;

Matthew 5:17 Think not that I am come to destroy the law or the prophets: I am not come to destroy, but to fulfill. 18. For verily I say unto you, Till heaven and earth pass, one jot or one tittle shall in no wise pass from the law, till all be fulfilled. 19. Whosoever, therefore, shall break one of these least commandments, <u>and shall teach men so</u>, he shall be called <u>the least</u> in the kingdom of heaven: but whosoever shall do and teach them, the same shall be called great in the kingdom of heaven.

Be careful, when you teach others that the commandments are done away and it is okay to break them, you become least in the Kingdom. Isn't our objective to make it to the Kingdom and be with Him? The universe and all the host within it operate by the rhythm of the Creator, and it is imperative that we begin to act within that rhythm. Who set the cycle of each week to seven days? Did man do it or was it the Creator? When we fail to observe the Sabbath, we lose the Most High's timing and direction for our lives. He created the weekly, monthly and yearly cycles. It is by his precise timing that we can regulate our days, months and years.

Chapter Eight: Insight into the Biblical New Year

We have discussed the weekly cycle, what about the months and the years? Each year on January 1, we celebrate with great enthusiasm the coming of the New Year. Our celebrations are jubilant, festive and sometimes riotous.

Churches celebrate by having a "watch night "service full of praise, prayer and worship. We count down to the new year in unity throughout the world. In New York, a ball is dropped and in most major cities in the United States there is fireworks. People kiss, hug and for a brief moment there appears to be love each for his fellow man.

What would you say if I told you that according to the Bible, January is not the star of the Biblical new year? Based upon what we know about how Sunday was changed; it is logical to think that we were lied to about the new year as well.

The sacred or ecclesiastical year begins in the month of Abib (March/April) and continues for twelve months. Hebrews use a calendar that is both lunar and solar. This combination helps to calculate the seasons of the year more accurately.

In the previous chapters we discussed how the enemy of the Hebrews sought to destroy us as a people. The quickest way was to do it was to dismantle our entire belief system.

The core of our existence was our belief in the Creator and His set of instructions called Torah. When we turned our backs to the Most High that was the beginning of our scattering and punishment. We were taken away by ships to every part of the world. (the Trans-Atlantic Slave Trade) Thus, fulfilling the book of Deuteronomy concerning our being scattered. So now we find ourselves sojourning in countries as the underclass, being mistreated and abused. But there is a bright shining light at the end of this gloomy tunnel.

We are in the process of awakening out of a deep sleep. Some of us have awakened sooner than others but, I believe it is just a matter of time and the world will know who we are.

Elohim is drawing us back to His calendar of events called the Feast Days. If we study them closely, He will unlock many of the Bible truths that were hidden from us in plain sight. One way to begin on this journey is to recognize the Biblical calendar and begin to observe His appointed times.

The Hebrew/Eber and Gregorian combination calendar:

https://www.bing.com/images/search?view=detailV2&id=636547C907B5E599676CFF4CC033B

When is His appointed times? The Bible is not ambiguous concerning the times that Elohim wants to meet. Using both the Gregorian and the Biblical calendar, we can figure out when they are. The main source that we will use is the King James Version of the Bible. The texts are found in the books of Exodus and Leviticus. We will also review the texts by using the Hebrew language to help bridge our understanding.

Exodus 12:1 And the LORD spake unto Moses and Aaron in the land of Egypt, saying, 2. This month shall be unto you the beginning of months: it shall be the first month of the year to you. 3. Speak ye unto all the congregation of Israel, saying, In the tenth day of this month they shall take to them every man a lamb, according to the house of their fathers, a lamb for a house:

The first thing that Elohim (God) spoke unto Moses was that a particular month would begin the year for Moses and the people of Israel. הַחֹדֶשׁ הַזֶּה □כֶם רֹאשׁ חֲדָשִׁים רִאשׁוֹן הוּא □כֶם □חָדְשֵׁי הַשָּׁנֶה:

The above Hebrew sentence reads the following;
"This month shall be unto you the beginning of month: it shall be the first month of the year to you."

The three phrases that have been highlighted in the above Hebrew sentence reading from left to right are (**Ha Chodosh הַחֹדֶשׁ**) which means "**this month**." The second group of words from this sentence is (**Rosh Chodoshim רֹאשׁ חֲדָשִׁים**) which means the head or **beginning of months**. Finally, the third phrase that is most important in this sentence is (**Rashon Le Chodosh Hashanah לְחָדְשֵׁי הַשָּׁנֶה רִאשׁוֹן**). The word <u>rashon</u> means <u>beginning or new</u>, le chadoshi means <u>of my months</u> and ha shanah means "ha" (the) and "shanah" (year).

The modern Ashkenazi Jews refer to the Feast of Trumpets as the new year (Rosh Ha Shanah). This confuses many people because the Bible clearly says something different. Aren't they the experts on the Torah?

As regathered Hebrews, it is imperative that we study the Torah for ourselves. We need to know when the New Year begin according to scripture. The Bible states that we are to begin our new year on His specified month. We find the name of that month in Exodus chapter 13 verse four. The month of Abib/Nisan is the beginning of the year or Rosh Ha Shanah.

Exodus 13:4 This day came ye out in the month Abib. הַיּוֹם אַתֶּם יֹצְאִים בְּחֹדֶשׁ הָאָבִיב:

This verse reads in Hebrew, ha yom (this day) atem (you plural) yotza'yim (came out plural) be Chodesh (in the month) ha Abib (the Abib).

What we understand from reading this passage is that the name of the month is called Abib. The month of Abib marks the beginning of a new year and the prelude to the first "Feast Day" of the new year.

Our next step is to understand as much as we can about Abib. Strong's 24 abib (הָאָבִיב) from an unused root meaning to be tender, green, a young ear of grain, ear, green ears of corn. The translators used the term corn; however, the proper reference should be barley.

The Hebrew word "Shiorah" (barley) derives its name from the long hairs (se'or) of its ears. In Biblical times, barley bread was the mainstay of the Israelite diet. The hardiness of the barley, especially in times of drought, made it the most important crop. It could be stored for long periods.

Barley was the first grain to ripen, and it symbolized the fact that spring was here. Barley also indicated that it was time for the first harvest of the new year. Abib or barley not only marked spring time, but helped to signal the preparation for the first "feast" of the year, Passover.

When the new moon of the green ears occurred, the spring

feasts were upon us. The Biblical spring Feasts are Passover, Unleavened Bread, Firstfruits and the Feast of Weeks. This is also considered a time to remember deliverance and freedom. On Passover, a lamb is slaughtered and prepared to be eaten that evening on the Feast of Unleavened Bread.

Unleavened bread is bread baked without leaven or yeast. The type of grain that they used to bake this unleavened bread was barley. The barley grain is also used for medicinal purposes. If you are suffering from medical conditions like obesity, constipation, diabetes, kidney problems or heart diseases, perhaps it's time for you to learn about the health benefits of barley. Barley has been said to have properties that aid in cleansing the body. During the Passover period, the Hebrews are commanded to cleanse their house of all leaven. During this same period, the Elohim (God) also prepared a cleansing for our bodies through barley that is used to bake the unleavened bread.

The name for barley in the Hebrew language is (sih orah) which sounds very similar to the word "Torah." If you break up the word for barley (se orah) you end up with two very unique words. The first part "se" is the word for lamb. The second part of the word (se orah) is the word orah which is the root of the word Torah. Could this word (se orah) be referring to the "lamb of the Torah?" Makes you say hmm.

When you insert yeast or leaven into the bread, it can be compared to "sin" because it causes the dough to puff up or rise. People who have too much pride and are considered puffed up or egotistic.

1 John 2:16 For all that is in the world, the lust of the flesh, and the lust of the eyes, and the pride of life, is not of the Father, but is of the world.

1Cor. 13:4 Charity suffered long, and *is kind; charity envied not; charity vaunted, not itself, is not puffed up,*

Col. 2:18 Let no man beguile you of your reward in a voluntary humility and worshipping of angels, intruding into those things which he hath not seen, vainly puffed up by his fleshly mind,

The bread referred to during this new year is not puffed up with the leavening agent. Could this be referring to a person?

Wheat, on the other hand, is used in making challah bread. The main ingredient in the Challah bread is leaven or yeast and eggs. The bread is allowed to sit until it rises and is twisted to form an interesting looking loaf. The loaf is baked until the top is slightly brown. It is very tasty and is sometimes sliced but usually the pieces are torn from the loaf. This is the bread of choice used during the typical Shabbat meal.

The Hebrew name for wheat is fascinating. Its name is "*Chittah*" Strong's 2406 which is of uncertain derivation, wheat, whether the grain or the plant. The Hebrew word "*chittah*" has the same two or three letter root and sounds quite similar to the Hebrew word that is translated as sin. The Hebrew word "*chattah*" means sin, offender or criminal.

Could It be that our understanding concerning leaven and sin came through the Hebrew correlation of leaven used in the baking of wheat? The leaven causes the bread to become puffed up (rise). The Challah bread looks and taste better than unleavened bread which is roasted on the hot fire. These two types of bread (barley and wheat) possibly represent two types of people. One chooses sin and the other choose to live righteously. The true meaning of the word Israel in Hebrew is Yasher El. The word "yasher" means to be upright. The word El is the shortened variation of the word Elohim which has been translated as the word (God). Yasher El is therefore, the "upright of God." It was Israel's mission to introduce YHWH to the world and have exemplary comportment.

We are to be obedient to His commandments, statutes and judgements. This includes, but not limited to observance of the Biblical appointed times.

Based upon the Scripture, the month of Abib begins a sacred New Year. The first ecclesiastical feast (appointed time) occur in this month. On some modern calendars, Abib was changed to Nisan. After careful investigation, we found that the name was changed after the Hebrews came out of Babylonian captivity. The name given to that month, biblically is Abib, not Nisan.

The Abib is barley grain when it is a light green color, firm, but not hard. When the barley grain was abib the first sighting of the next new moon indicated the start of the first day of the first month of a new year. The Passover is always in the Spring in the month of the Abib. This is the same month that our forefathers came out of Egypt.

Exodus 12:24 And ye shall observe this thing for an ordinance to thee and to thy sons forever. 25. And it shall come to pass, when ye be come to the land which the LORD will give you, according as he hath promised, that ye shall keep this service. 26. and it shall come to pass, when your children shall say unto you, what mean ye by this service? 27. hat ye shall say, it is the sacrifice of the LORD'S Passover, who passed over the houses of the children of Israel in Egypt, when he smote the Egyptians, and delivered our houses. And the people bowed the head and worshipped.

Exodus 13:8 And thou shalt shew thy son in that day, saying, This is done because of that which the LORD did unto me when I came forth out of Egypt. 9. And it shall be for a sign unto thee upon thine hand, and for a memorial between thine eyes, that the LORD'S law may be in thy mouth: for with a strong hand hath the LORD brought thee out of Egypt. 10. Thou shalt therefore keep this ordinance in his season from year to year.

Deuteronomy 6:6 And these words, which I command thee this day, shall be in thine heart: 7. And thou shalt teach them diligently unto thy children, and shalt talk of them when thou sittest in thine house, and when thou walkest by the way, and when thou liest down, and when thou risest up.

The Elohim (God) promised Israel that when they came into the land that it would be good and would have brooks of water with fountains that spring out of the valleys and hills. He also promised seven species of plants, wheat, barley, vines (grapes), fig trees, pomegranates, olives and oil from the olives and honey.

We have shown the importance of barley and wheat and how they relate to "Torah and sin." Let's take a closer look at another of the seven species, "figs." The Hebrew name of this fruit (Strong's 8384) "te an" which means to lie or become naughty. This word fig refers to the garden of Eden when Adam and his wife had sinned (chattah) and covered themselves up with fig leaves.

Genesis 3:6 And when the woman saw that the tree was good for food and that it was pleasant to the eyes, and a tree to be desired to make one wise, she took of the fruit thereof, and did eat, and gave also unto her husband with her; and he did eat. 7. And the eyes of them both were opened, and they knew that they were naked, and they sewed fig leaves together and made themselves aprons. 8. And they heard the voice of the LORD God walking in the garden in the cool of the day: and Adam and his wife hid from the presence of the LORD God amongst the trees of the garden. 9. And the LORD God

~ 73 ~

called unto Adam, and said unto him, Where art thou? 10. And he said, I heard thy voice in the garden, and I was afraid because I was naked, and I hid myself. 11. And he said, who told thee that thou wast naked? Hast thou eaten of the tree, whereof I commanded thee that thou shouldest not eat? 12. And the man said, the woman whom thou gavest to be with me, she gave me of the tree, and I did eat.

It is interesting that another of the seven species that Israel would receive was a reminder of the sin in the garden. The leaves of the fig tree were used to "cover" their nakedness or sin. The Elohim (God) reminded them that you could not use what comes out of the dirt to cover your dirt (sin). The Elohim took an innocent animal, slaughtered that animal shedding its "blood" and used the skin of that animal as a cover for Adam's nakedness (sin). It was evident in the garden experience that the remedy for sin would have to be blood.

The seven species are listed below:

Wheat, Strong's 2406, (chittah) of uncertain derivation, which means wheat, whether the grain or the plant, puffed up with leaven. Chattah, sin, miss the mark.

Barley Strong's 8184, (Sehorah) the barley grain, in the sense of roughness, the plant, also sounds similar to (T' orah) light.

Vine - Strong's 1612, (G' phen) to bend, vine, the grape, tree, wine.

Fig Tree - Strong's 8384, (T' an) to lie, naughty.

Pomegranates - Strong's 7416, (Remmown) from 7426 ramam – prim root to rise, exalt, get up, lift up, upright, the tree, fruit.

Olive Strong's 2132, (zayith) akin to 2099, brightness, flowers, illuminating oil, the tree, the branch or berry.

HoneyStrong's 1706, (de bash) to be gummy, sticky, syrup, honey (comb) symbol of protection and resurrection, healing of wounds.

There appears to be a hidden message in the seven species that the Elohim (God) promised Israel. When you place all the Hebrew definitions together, there is a profound message.

"The puffed up (wheat) plant or people that missed the mark would be cleansed (barley) through the Torah, the blood and wine to remedy the lie of sin and darkness, causing you to rise up and stand upright. The illuminating oil of the spirit will lead you back into the tree that you came from causing you to become a symbol of resurrection, protection, and healing of wounds."

Chapter Nine: The Tenth Day Lamb

Exodus 12:3 Speak ye unto all the congregation of Israel, saying, In the tenth day of this month they shall take to them every man a lamb, according to the house of their fathers, a lamb for a house:

We now understand that the "New Year" was to begin in the month of Abib. We also know that the Hebrew language is concise and tells you exactly what to do. Because of the construct of the Hebrew language, where the letters have names, sounds, meanings, and numbers, scriptures can efficiently be coded with hidden meanings, as previously demonstrated.

Prov. 25:2 It is the glory of God to conceal a thing: but the honor of kings is to search out a matter.

The Feasts of Yahweh are His Feasts. Most people think that the Feasts belong to the European Jews. That is far from being accurate. Mainly when you read the term (Jew) in the Brit Hadashah (New Testament), people automatically think of the European Jews of today. That also is inaccurate! The people of the Book were called Hebrews and were not Europeans. That term "Jew" is a transliteration of the word Yehuda or (Judah).

The people of the Book remained in Africa. They were very dark, and some were brown skinned. It saddens me to have to discuss the color issue. But the Ashkenazi has attempted to replace the original Hebrews by suggesting they are the ones called Hebrew/Eber. Over 90% of the Caucasian Jews of the world are Ashkenazi. Ashkenazi was the grandson of the gentile Japheth. He was the founder of the gentiles who were Germans, Russians, Greeks, Italians and the Finnish. They converted and adopted Hebrew as a religion through the

Talmud. I am not trying to offend anyone; I am just telling the truth. We can be brothers but don't try to replace us.

The scripture declare that the Feasts belongs to Yah and Him only. These Feast Days are neither Jew, Christian or Muslim. He set the dates and times, and all He asked us to do is to meet Him. His feast days were significant because they were types and shadows of things to come.

Lev. 23:2 Speak unto the children of Israel, and say unto them, Concerning the feasts of the LORD, which ye shall proclaim to be holy convocations, even these are my feasts.

Why did He say to Moses to get a lamb on the 10th day? What was the significance of that? Why the tenth day and why a lamb? Remember the Hebrew term for barley (se orah) denotes a lamb (she) hidden within the word. Is it coincident that the spring was the time of the barley season and the birthing of the lamb during the same time?

Isa. 46:10 Declaring the end from the beginning, and from ancient times the things that are not yet done, saying, My counsel shall stand, and I will do all my pleasure:

We must understand that He has always been in full control. He is omniscient which means he knows the end from the beginning and everything in between. We must also be aware that everything in the book points to Yahshua/Jesus.

John 5:39 Search the scriptures; for in them ye think ye have eternal life: and they are they which testify of me.

The Book of John in the "New Testament" was written around 85 AD which was over 50 years after the death of Yahshua. My question to you is what the scripture that Yahshua was referring to if the "New Testament" had not even been written was? The answer is simple, the Torah, the Writings, and the Prophets. All the writings in the so-called "Old Testament" pointed to, alluded to or spoke directly about Yahshua.

Therefore, if a lamb was to be chosen on the tenth day and brought to the house, what does that have to do with Yahshua? Once you begin reading the scripture from a Hebraic perspective, the Bible narratives will become more apparent to you. Moses was instructed to tell the people to get a lamb and bring him to the house on the 10th day of the month of Abib.

The Lamb:
Why did the animal have to be a lamb? Upon careful investigation about sheep, we found that sheep mate in the fall and lambs are born in the spring when the weather is mild, and the grass is plentiful. This scenario offers the best opportunity for the lambs to survive and thrive.

Sheep are also known for their strong flocking behaviors. They have a strong instinct for following. When they are frightened, they will run. Their instinct also makes them aware that there is safety in numbers, so they band together in groups for their protection. It is easier for a predator to catch a wandering sheep or lamb when they have strayed from the group.

Another exciting thing about sheep is that they look for a leader. At birth, lambs are taught to follow the older more experienced members of the flock. The dominant ones usually lead the others who are less assertive. The ram in the herd is often the leader. Sheep have excellent hearing. They can pinpoint sound with their sensitive hearing. Sudden and loud noises such as barking dogs and unnatural sounds will frighten the sheep and make them nervous. It is said that the handler of the sheep should speak to them in a calm, quiet voice. The questions are, "what does this have to do with Yahshua?

First of all, Yahshua called His people the sheep of His pasture. It was through the sense of hearing that sin entered the world through Adam and Eve. The first family listened to the voice of the serpent in the garden, and we now continue in that vein by listening to the wrong voice.

Gen. 3:1 Now the serpent was more subtle than any beast of the field which the LORD God had made. And he said unto the woman, Yea, hath God said, Ye shall not eat of every tree of the garden? 2. And the woman said unto the serpent, we may eat of the fruit of the trees of the garden: 3. But of the fruit of the tree which is in the midst of the garden, God hath said, Ye shall not eat of it, neither shall ye touch it, lest ye die. 4. And the serpent said unto the woman, Ye shall not surely die 5. For God doth know that in the day ye eat thereof, then your eyes shall be opened, and ye shall be as gods, knowing good and evil. 6. And when the woman saw that the tree was good for food and that it was pleasant to the eyes, and a tree to be desired to make one wise, she took of the fruit thereof, and did eat, and gave also unto her husband with her; and he did eat. 7. And the eyes of them both were opened, and they knew that they were naked, and they sewed fig leaves together and made themselves aprons.

When our forefathers listened to the wrong voice in the garden, sin (lust of the flesh, the lust of eye and pride of life) entered the world all through the sense of hearing the wrong voice. Therefore, the remedy for our sins will be from the same sense of hearing which is what led to sin in the first place. Yahshua said that His sheep hear his voice and another they will not follow. What it took to start will be what it takes to finish.

Roman 10:13 For whosoever shall call upon the name of the Lord shall be saved. 14. How then shall they call on him in whom they have not believed? and how shall they believe in him of whom they have not heard? and how shall they hear without a preacher? 15. And how shall they preach, except they be sent? as it is written, how beautiful are the feet of them that preach the gospel of peace and bring glad tidings of good things! 17. So then faith *cometh* by hearing and hearing by the word of God.

The Bible refers to Yahshua as a messianic lamb. When John the Baptizer saw Yahshua, he did not see his cousin anymore, nor did he see a man, he saw a lamb.

John 1:29 The next day John seeth Yahshua (Jesus) coming unto him, and saith, Behold the Lamb of God, which taketh away the sin of the world.

Do we read that passage of scripture without questioning why did John only see a lamb? He could have mentioned a cow or a bird, but he saw a lamb. John also knew the scriptures concerning the instructions that were given to Moses to gather a lamb on the tenth day.

Exodus 12:3 Speak ye unto all the congregation of Israel, saying, In the tenth day of this month they shall take to them every man a lamb, according to the house of their fathers, a lamb for a house:

John was a Nazarene, and his father was a priest and performed duties in the temple. I am sure that he was well versed in scripture and he did not accidentally call Yahshua a lamb.

So, what is the significance of the 10th day? First of all, in the scenario being played out in Exodus, the number 10 also refers to the last plague of Egypt which was the death of the firstborn. The Elohim (God) is sovereign and can do whatever He chooses, but we also know that He is specific and does not do anything by happenstance.

The lamb was selected and brought to the house on the tenth day to be befriended and examined by the family. They were instructed to keep the lamb at home until the 14th day. Is it possible that the same thing happened to Yahshua? Let's take a closer look!

John 12:1 Then Jesus six days before the Passover came to Bethany, where Lazarus was which had been dead, whom he raised from the dead. 2. There they made him a supper, and Martha served: but Lazarus was one of them that sat at the table with him. Verse 12. On the next day much people that were come to the feast, when they heard that Jesus was coming to Jerusalem,

Why was this event so important? The scripture indicates that he arrived at Bethany six days before Passover. Passover occurred on the 14th day of the month of Abib. Six days prior would be on the 8th day of the month of Abib. Moses instructed them to get a lamb on the 10th day of Abib and bring it to the house. We know that Yahshua arrived in Bethany on the 8th day. John 12:12 also tells us that Yahshua spent the night and the next day set out to go to Jerusalem.

Luke 19 provides even more clarity regarding what we call the "Triumphal Entry."

Luke 19:29 And it came to pass when he was come nigh to Bethpage and Bethany, at the mount called the mount of Olives, he sent two of his disciples, 30. Saying, Go ye into the village over against you; in the which at your entering ye shall find a colt tied, whereon yet never man sat: loose him, and bring him hither. 31. And if any man asks you, why do ye loose him? thus shall ye say unto him, Because the Lord hath need of him. 32. And they that were sent went their way and found even as he had said unto them. 33. And as they were loosing the colt, the owners thereof said unto them, Why loose ye the colt? 34. And they said The Lord (YHWH) hath need of him. 35.

And they brought him to Jesus: and they cast their garments upon the colt, and they set Jesus thereon. 36. And as he went, they spread their clothes in the way. 37. And when he was come nigh, even now at the descent of the mount of Olives, the whole multitude of the disciples began to rejoice and praise God with a loud voice for all the mighty works that they had seen. 38. Saying, blessed be the King that cometh in the name of the Lord: peace in heaven, and glory in the highest.

The village of Bethpage on the Mount of Olives was a most important religious center for the Judahite authorities in the period of the Messiah and the apostles. The word "Bethpage" means the "House of Unripe Figs." It was no accident that the Messiah told his disciples to go into Bethpage and obtain a donkey for him to ride into Jerusalem to fulfill the prophecy of Zechariah about the Judahites adoring their king riding on a donkey. The prediction was fulfilled concerning Jacob as he was blessing his son Judah;

Genesis 49:9 Judah is a lion's whelp: from the prey, my son, thou art gone up: he stooped down, he couched as a lion, and as an old lion; who shall rouse him up? 10. The scepter shall not depart from Judah, nor a lawgiver from between his feet, until Shiloh come; and unto him shall the gathering of the people be. 11. Binding his foal unto the vine, and his ass's colt unto the choice vine; he washed his garments in wine, and his clothes in the blood of grapes:

However, wait, there is more! According to the instructions given to Moses, they brought the lamb to the house during that time. Let's look at Matt. 21 and see what happened.

Matt. 21:10 And when he has come into Jerusalem, all the city was moved, saying, who is this? 11. And the multitude said this is Jesus the prophet of Nazareth of Galilee. 12. And Jesus went into the temple of God, and cast out all them that sold and bought in the

temple, and overthrew the tables of the moneychangers, and the seats
of them that sold doves, 13. And said unto them, It is written, <u>My</u>
<u>house</u> shall be called the <u>house</u> of prayer, but ye have made it a den
of thieves.

The first place Yahshua went was to the Temple or His house
on the tenth day. He was there following the instructions
given to Moses. Another key factor is that He was given the
title "the Lamb that taketh away the Sin of the world." What
did John mean by using the term "Sin" versus sins? There is a
remarkable distinction between Sin and sins. Let's review the
book of Mark 11.

Mark 11:12 And on the morrow, when they were come from
Bethany, he was hungry: 13. And seeing a <u>fig tree afar off</u>
<u>having leaves,</u> he came, if haply he might find anything
thereon: and when he came to it, he found nothing but leaves;
for the time of figs was not *yet*. 14. And Jesus answered and
said unto it, no man eat the fruit of thee hereafter forever. And
his disciples heard *it*.

This scripture is fundamental. Most of us are aware that after
the "Sin" entered the world, Adam and Eve ate of the fruit of the
tree of Knowledge of good and evil and knew that they were
naked. In an attempt to hide the shame of their nakedness, they
sewed "fig leaves" together and covered their body parts that
were exposed.

Yahshua cursed a particular fig tree which had only leaves and
no fruit. He then spoke to the tree and said, "no man eat the
fruit of thee hereafter forever." Was Yahshua speaking about
an unyielding tree or was He speaking to the curse of sin that
was set upon man by them attempting to hide their sin with fig
leaves. What we do know is that every element that contributed
to "the Sin" from the garden was dealt with by Him.

Exodus 12:3 Speak ye unto all the congregation of Israel, saying, In the tenth day of this month they shall take to them every man a lamb, according to the house of their fathers, a lamb for a home: 4. And if the household is too little for the lamb, let him and his neighbor next unto his house take it according to the number of the souls; every man according to his eating shall make your count for the lamb. 5. Your lamb shall be without blemish, a male of the first year: ye shall take it out from the sheep, or the goats:

They brought the lamb to the house. What a great picture that Yahshua was casting out money changers declaring that His "house" was a "house" of prayer, but they made it a den of thieves. We also disclosed how Yahshua fulfilled the prophecy that Jacob made to Judah concerning the colts that were tied and how He cursed the fig tree which represented our attempts to cover sin. However, the instructions given to Moses were more specific. The lamb had to meet certain qualifications and specifications. The lamb had to be examined and found without spot or blemish. He also had to be a male of the 1st year.

Exodus 12:5 5. Your lamb shall be without blemish, a male of the first year: ye shall take it out from the sheep, or the goats:

I searched to see if Yahshua met those qualifications. It was not surprising that the scriptures confirmed that He did. The writer, John's witness, was reliable because it was divinely inspired. He saw the totality of the divine holiness of Yahshua by declaring He not only had the ability but He also the right to take away the "Sin" of the world. That was a compelling revelation that John received.

However, who examined Yahshua and checked out his credentials for Him to qualify as the lamb? Let's take a closer look at the scripture to see if there were some clues or actual testimonies of people that examined him.

Luke 22:66 And as soon as it was day, the elders of the people and the chief priests and the scribes came together, and led him into their council, saying 67. Art thou the Christ? tell us. And he said unto them, If I tell you, ye will not believe: 68. And if I also ask you, ye will not answer me, nor let me go. 69. Hereafter shall the Son of man sit on the right hand of the power of God. 70. Then said they all, Art thou then the Son of God? And he said unto them, Ye say that I am. 71. And they said, what need we any further witness? for we ourselves have heard of his own mouth.

According to the Book of Luke, the elders of the people, the chief priests, and scribes all came together against Him to examine Him. The Prophet Isaiah wrote that this would eventually happen. Did the disciples and others know that the scripture was being fulfilled right before their very eyes?

Isaiah 53:7 He was oppressed, and he was afflicted, yet he opened not his mouth: he is brought as a lamb to the slaughter, and as a sheep, before her shearers is dumb, so he openeth not his mouth.

Luke 23 goes on to say that the one that had authority above the Sanhedrin was to examine Him as well. Pilate also passed a judgment rendering Yahshua without spot or blemish.

Luke 23:1 And the whole multitude of them arose and led him unto Pilate. 2. And they began to accuse him, saying, we found this fellow perverting the nation, and forbidding to give tribute to Caesar, saying that he himself is Christ a King. 3. And Pilate asked him, saying, Art thou the King of the Jews? And he answered him and said, Thou sayest it. 4. Then said Pilate to the chief priests and to the people, I find no fault in this man.

Pilate questioned Him as to whether Yahshua was King of the Yahudi. However, Yahshua answered Pilate and said, "That is what you say." Pilate also received a divine revelation right at that moment and declared Yahshua to without fault. The Prophet Isaiah's prophecy was fulfilled that said, "He had done no violence, nor was any wickedness found in his mouth." To get a better understanding, you should read the entire 53rd book of Isaiah. Although He suffered great injustice, He still was depicted as sinless. HalleluYah.

Revelation 5:8 And when he had taken the book, the four beasts and four and twenty elders fell before the Lamb, having every one of them harps, and golden vials full of odors, which are the prayers of saints. 9. And they sang a new song, saying, Thou art worthy to take the book, and to open the seals thereof: for thou wast slain, and hast redeemed us to Elohim (God) by thy blood out of every kindred, and tongue, and people, and nation; 10. And hast made us unto our Elohim (God) kings and priests: and we shall reign on the earth.

It is evident that Yahshua's timely arrival to His house on the 10th day fulfilled the instructions that were by the prophets and Moses. We also know that He was examined but was found blameless.

Chapter Ten: Understanding Passover

Ex. 12:6 And ye shall keep it up until the fourteenth day of the same month: and the whole assembly of the congregation of Israel shall kill it at twilight.

According to Exodus chapter 12, the people of Israel were instructed to keep the lamb until the 14th day. As we discussed in the section on "time" the 14th day in the lunar calendar always has a full moon. We talked earlier about the sun, moon, and stars being a signal or sign for the Feast Days of Yah. The term "sign" in Hebrew is the word "owth."

oht
(The Sign, or The Seal)

vav Nail, tent peg, to secure, "and"

tav Cross, covenant (or sign of the covenant)

אות

alef Ox, bull; strength, leader, first
The Jews also see this letter as the letter representing God!

https://www.bing.com/images/search?q=Owth+Hebrew&FORM=IRBPRS&=0

To reiterate, the word Owth is comprised of the Hebrew letters, "alef, vav and tav". The alef is depicted as an ox head and means strong, and the vav is depicted as a nail or peg which connects. Finally, the picture of the tav is a cross which means covenant. If you put the meaning of all three letters together, it should read, "The strong one nailed to the covenant cross." Again, what an breathtaking picture of what would happen in the future during Passover!

Ex. 12:6 And ye shall keep it up until the fourteenth day of the same month: and the whole assembly of the congregation of Israel shall kill it at twilight.

According to the instructions given to Moses in Exo. 12:6, on the 14th day they had to slaughter the lamb at twilight. In many Bibles, the time is referred to as either twilight or evening. Check your Bible to see which word is translated.

Most people read the word "twilight," and gloss over it as if it has nothing to do with the sentence. The fact is, the word "Twilight" is the most critical word in that sentence. Earlier we discussed the fact that dates and times are essential to Yah and He does not need to use words as fillers. The Hebrew language is clear and concise. When the Elohim (God) says something, He means what He says and says what He means.

So, what does Twilight mean? The word or prefix "twi" means two. The meaning of light in this word is "mid-day." The entire word (twilight) means between the two lights. The question is what two lights? The Samaritans and the Pharisees held two prevailing views.

The Pharisees held the view that the last quarter of the daylight portion of the day, before sunset, was called twilight. This view is supported in historical references such as Josephus and the Bible, Mathew 27:46, 57 and Mark 15:34,42.

In the New Testament, the first evening is referenced as the 9th hour of the day. The second evening was at sunset. The Samaritans and Karaites held the latter view. Before dark or 6:00 and after mid-day. The brightest light during the day is at mid-day or noon. Nightfall in that part of the world is at approximately 6:00. Therefore, twilight occurred between 12:00 mid-day and 6:00 night fall.

Luke 23:44 And it was about the sixth hour, and there was a darkness over all the earth until the ninth hour.

Matt. 27:45 Now from the sixth hour there was darkness over all the land unto the ninth hour.

Mark 15:34, 42 And at the ninth hour Jesus cried with a loud voice, saying, Eloi, Eloi, lama sabachthani? which is, being interpreted, My God, my God, why hast thou forsaken me?

The first light begins at 6:00 am which is usually dawn in that part of the word. Therefore, the sixth hour is our noon mid-day and comprise the most illuminous part of the day. The ninth hour is 3:00 in the afternoon. Finally, at 6:00 pm represent evening which is the close of the daylight hours.

When the Catholic church adopted the concept of "Good Friday" they used the aforementioned scriptures to determine the time that they would hold their mass. Most churches that follow the Catholic tradition of "Good Friday," continue the tradition by holding their meetings from noon mid-day to the 3:00 hour. So why does the entire Christian body choose to hold their "Good Friday" services at those hours? Did they know that the Hebrews were observing the Passover sacrifice at the exact same time? Of course, they knew! YHWH instructed Moses to kill or slaughter the Passover lamb at twilight. This is the same time period that the Roman Catholic church used when they established "Good Friday." Which observance came first, "Passover or Good Friday?" I will let you figure out the answer.

The Hebrew term for killed is Strong's 7819 (shachat) a prim root to slaughter, offer or slay. Also, with the idea of "hammer out, striking or beating. The prophet Isaiah saw Him wounded, bruised and striped.

Isa. 53:5 But he was wounded for our transgressions, he was bruised for our iniquities: the chastisement of our peace was upon him; and with his stripes we are healed.

The key to understanding how the lamb was slaughtered, is found in the method used for shedding the blood. They drained the slaughtered animal's blood into a basin. Then they took hyssop, dipped it in the basin or pan. Finally, they took the blood that was on the hyssop and applied it the lintel (top of the door) and the two side posts of the door. I am certain no one was aware that this act was the preliminary picture of Yahshua being hung on the cross.

If you look close at the image of the door below you see blood at the top and sides. Draw a line from the blood on the lintel (top portion of the door) to the floor and draw a line across from each bloody post to post, you will see the image of a cross. If you use your imagination, you will also see the what appears to be blood from a man's head on the lintel and blood from his hands on the two side posts.

https://www.bing.com/images/search?q=blood%20on%20the%20lintel%20and%20two%20sid

The Image that you should have seen is the image of a man suspended on a stake or cross with his hands nailed to the crossbars, and His head was bleeding on the lintel of the door. What a picture!

When Moses was instructed to make sure all the Children of Israel applied blood to the doorposts, did Moses also see the image we are seeing? Just a thought.

Exodus 12:22 And ye shall take a bunch of hyssops and dip it in the blood that is in the basin and strike the lintel and the two side posts with the blood that is in the pan, and none of you shall go out at the door of his house until the morning.

23. For the LORD will pass through to smite the Egyptians; and when he seeth the blood upon the lintel, and on the two side posts, the LORD will pass over the door, and will not suffer the destroyer to come in unto your houses to smite you.

Hyssop:

We know that blood is the remedy for sin, but Yahshua had the task of following the instructions exactly the way it was prescribed to Moses. The Bible mentions hyssop several times, mostly in the "Old Testament."

In Leviticus 14:1-7 the Elohim (God) commanded His people to use hyssop in the ceremonial cleansing of people and houses. In one example, Elohim (God) tells the priest to use hyssop together with cedar wood, scarlet yarn, and the blood of a clean bird to sprinkle a person recently healed from a skin disease (likely leprosy). This act would ceremonially cleanse the formerly diseased person and allow him to re-enter the camp. The same method was used to purify a house that had previously contained mold. (Leviticus 14:33-53)

David mentioned hyssop in *Psalm 51:7 "cleanse me with hyssop, and I will be clean; wash me, and I will be whiter than snow."* David was not referring to a physical cleansing, but instead asking the Elohim to cleanse him morally as he confessed his sins. Hyssop was used symbolically in the Bible. When the Israelites marked their doorposts with the lamb's blood before Elohim passing over the land, Elohim instructed them to use a bunch of hyssops as a "paintbrush" (Exodus 12:22). Hyssop was sturdy and could withstand the brushing.

It is also very likely that Elohim was marking His people as being pure or cleansed. Anyone that was on the inside of the blood markings as saved from the 10th plague judgment that was being poured out on the Egyptians and those that were disobedient to Moses's instructions.

The lintel of the door is called the header panel. Let's see what happened to Yahshua. Were the instructions carried out?

John 19:29 Now there was set a vessel full of vinegar: and they filled a sponge with vinegar, and put it upon hyssop, and put it to his mouth. 30. When Yahshua (Jesus) therefore had received the vinegar, he said, it is finished: and he bowed his head, and gave up the ghost.

They took the hyssop, with sour wine (blood) and put it up to Yahshua's mouth (header panel). Please note that Yahshua cried out the during the same time, the exact statement that the High Priest would cry out after he slaughtered the last lamb. He broadcast to the crowd, "It is Finished."

But I have greater witness than that of John: for the works which the Father hath given me to finish, the same works that I do, bear witness of me, that the Father hath sent me.

The priests and the people would conclude the ceremony by singing the Hallel hymn. The last part of the hymn, speaks to tying the sacrifice to the altar;

Psalm 118:24 This is the day which the LORD hath made; we will rejoice and be glad in it. 25. Save now; I beseech thee, O LORD: O LORD, I beseech thee, send now prosperity. 26. Blessed be he that cometh in the name of the LORD: we have blessed you out of the house of the LORD. 27 Elohim (God) is the LORD, which hath shewed us light: bind the sacrifice with cords, even unto the horns of the altar. 28. Thou art my Elohim (God), and I will praise thee:

thou art my Elohim (God), I will exalt thee. 29. O give thanks unto the LORD; for he is good: for his mercy endured forever.

During one of our previous chapters, we discussed the 10th day and its meaning. We showed how Yahshua came into Jerusalem riding on a donkey (like a king) fulfilling what was written in the book of Zechariah. There are seven feasts which begin with the Feast of Passover or Pesach. The crucifixion occurred on Passover and is now observed throughout most of the modern world.

Crucifixion Week Abib 31 C.E.

Feasts of YaHuWaH in Leviticus 23

Yah's day begins from evening and goes to evening (sunset to sunset)

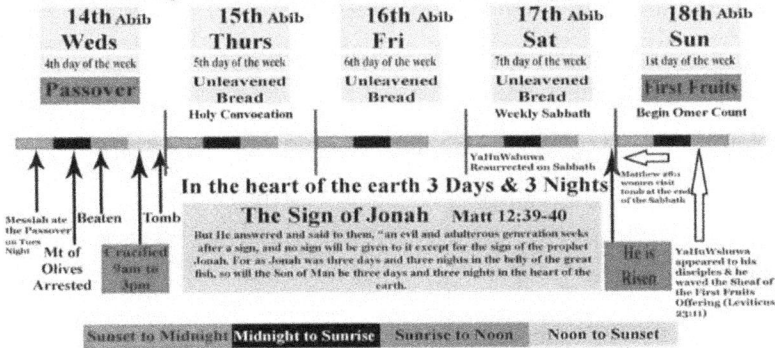

14th Abib	15th Abib	16th Abib	17th Abib	18th Abib
Weds	**Thurs**	**Fri**	**Sat**	**Sun**
4th day of the week	5th day of the week	6th day of the week	7th day of the week	1st day of the week
Passover	Unleavened Bread	Unleavened Bread	Unleavened Bread	First Fruits
	Holy Convocation		Weekly Sabbath	Begin Omer Count

YaHuWshuwa Resurrected on Sabbath

In the heart of the earth 3 Days & 3 Nights

Matthew 28:1 women visit tomb at the end of the Sabbath

Messiah ate the Passover on Tues Night — Mt of Olives Arrested | Beaten | Tomb | Crucified 9am to 3pm | He is Risen

The Sign of Jonah Matt 12:39-40

But He answered and said to them, "an evil and adulterous generation seeks after a sign, and no sign will be given to it except for the sign of the prophet Jonah. For as Jonah was three days and three nights in the belly of the great fish, so will the Son of Man be three days and three nights in the heart of the earth.

YaHuWshuwa appeared to his disciples & he waved the Sheaf of the First Fruits Offering (Leviticus 23:11)

Sunset to Midnight | Midnight to Sunrise | Sunrise to Noon | Noon to Sunset

Chapter Eleven: The Week of Blood

It is problematic that the Catholic Church invented the concept of "Good Friday." They changed the day of the actual crucifixion to a Friday to occur every year. They also scheduled "Good Friday" so that the Sunday following, would consistently be the celebration of Easter.

It was clever to schedule Good Friday during this time, but something nefarious was lurking in the background. They also inserted the name of a pagan goddess, Ishtar, Easter or Ashtaroth instead of the Feast of Firstfruits. Where did the name Easter come from? The name Easter comes from an ancient Babylonian goddess named Ishtar. Ishtar was the name of the counterpart to Baal.

The Roman emperor Constantine was a worshipper of the sun god Mithrias. He syncretized the worship of the sun with the religion of Christianity and ordered his empire to honor the day of the resurrection of Yahshua / Jesus, as Easter.

Legend states that after Semiramis died, she ascended to the heavens and eventually fell back to earth, landing in the Euphrates in an egg. It is said that a dove help push her to land where she incarnated. For helping her, she changed the dove into a rabbit or bunny. Thus, we have the tradition of hunting for "Easter" eggs and bunnies. They added Easter egg hunts, egg dyeing, and other pagan customs to the celebration of the resurrection.

Passover involves the death of the lamb, and we already discussed that John branded Yahshua as the "Lamb of Elohim (God)."

During the time that Yahshua lived, Passover occurred on a

Wednesday or the 4th day of the week. Review the calendar on the illustration below:

https://www.bing.com/images/search?q=The%20crucifixion%20week&c

Crucifixion Week Abib 31 C.E.
Feasts of YaHuWaH in Leviticus 23
Yah's day begins from evening and goes to evening (sunset to sunset)

14th Abib	15th Abib	16th Abib	17th Abib	18th Abib
Weds	Thurs	Fri	Sat	Sun
4th day of the week	5th day of the week	6th day of the week	7th day of the week	1st day of the week
Passover	Unleavened Bread	Unleavened Bread	Unleavened Bread	First Fruits
	Holy Convocation		Weekly Sabbath	Begin Omer Count

In the heart of the earth 3 Days & 3 Nights

The Sign of Jonah   Matt 12:39-40

But He answered and said to them, "an evil and adulterous generation seeks after a sign, and no sign will be given to it except for the sign of the prophet Jonah. For as Jonah was three days and three nights in the belly of the great fish, so will the Son of Man be three days and three nights in the heart of the earth.

Sunset to Midnight Midnight to Sunrise Sunrise to Noon Noon to Sunset

bir=sbi&imageBin=&qs=n&form

Using the illustrated calendar, the day of Passover (the sacrifice of the Lamb) was on Wednesday. If you count backward six days starting on Wednesday, you end up on Thursday the week before, being the day that Yahshua arrived in Bethany.

He enjoyed a meal with Lazarus and his family. The next morning, he got up and headed toward Jerusalem. Jerusalem was about 3 hours or less in travel time from Bethany. He arrived in Jerusalem on Friday, when the currency exchange and purchase of sacrifices occurred because the following day was Sabbath.

His entry to Jerusalem, he was honored by the people who threw down palm branches before him and recited the last part of the hymn called the "Hallel" (Psalm 118). During that time, He also cursed the fig tree.

Yahshua did not curse the fig tree haphazardly. He did it because it represented the original sin of Adam and Eve. The two of them used fig leaves to cover their nakedness or sin.

Elohim would not accept the leaves from this tree as a covering for their bodies and sin. Elohim took the skin or hide from an innocent animal to cover them.

Yahshua declared that the leaves from that fig tree could no longer be used to cover sin, only the blood of the crucified one! He confronted man's attempt to hide sin in the garden of Eden. We still try to cover our sins with lies and deceitfulness.

The next day was Sabbath the 10th day of Abib. Yahshua taught in the temple, and He stayed near the Temple (house) teaching until the 14th day. Four days later in the middle of the week on the 4th day of the week specifically at twilight, He was crucified.

How interesting is it that the sun, moon, and stars were created on the 4th day of the creation week, the 14th day of Abib occurred on the 4th day of the week of the Crucifixion?

The Elohim (God) instructed Moses to make the Menorah. (Candlestick) The menorah lit up the second most Holy Place in the Tabernacle. This Menorah had seven branches. He made the Menorah from pure beaten gold. In other words, there was no soldering together pieces. The Menorah was beaten out from one piece. The Hebrew term "beaten" meant to be made "upright." It had bowls with wicks for the oil to light the Menorah.

It is said that each of the seven branches represented one of the days of creation and one thousand years. The fourth branch was called the servant branch. Each of the branches represents a thousand years, and the fourth stem was called the "servant branch. It is not coincidental that Yahshua lived during the 4th millennium. Could there be a pattern here?

In the Bible, the first sentence that you read uses 7 Hebrew words;

בְּרֵאשִׁית בָּרָא אֱלֹהִים אֵת הַשָּׁמַיִם וְאֵת הָאָרֶץ:

Notice that I highlighted the fourth word. The first letter of that word is Aleph and the second letter of the word is tav. The first Paleo Hebrew letter aleph is depicted an ox or rams head.   It meant strong and powerful. The second letter tav was shaped like a cross and meant covenant. The Aleph is the first letter in the Hebrew aleph-bet and the tav is the last letter.

The 4th Hebrew word in our Bible, (Aleph/Tav), meant "strong covenant or the strong one's cross."

Rev. 1:8 I am Alpha (Aleph) and Omega (tav), the beginning and the ending, saith the Lord, which is, and which was, and which is to come, the Almighty.

Yahshua declared that He was the, "first and last." This phrase was used six times in the book of Revelation. We can, therefore, conclude that the 4th word in our Bible "aleph / tav" is a code denoting Yahshua. He lived during the fourth millennium and was slaughtered or killed on the 4th day of the week. There are also four letters in the name YHWH. This is not a coincidence; it was a slight observation into how Elohim used numerical sequences to bring forth his magnificent plan.

Do you remember when, the writer John named Yahshua the "Lamb of God?" This was also not done by chance. John did not see Yahshua as a man, he saw him as a sacrificial lamb. This lamb had to be examined before he was killed. In the course of time, the elders, scribes, Pharisees, and Pilate all examined Him. But in the end, the highest authority of that land declared that He was without fault!

Luke 23:4 Then said Pilate to the chief priests and to the people, I find no fault in this man.

John 18:38 Pilate saith unto him, "What is truth?" And when he had said this, he went again unto the Hebrews, and saith unto them, I find in him no fault at all.

John 19:4 Pilate therefore went forth again and saith unto them, Behold, I bring him forth to you, that ye may know that I find no fault in him.

The process that they used to offer an animal on the surface appeared a bit gruesome. The lamb was slaughtered in a prescribed manner called "Shachat." Shachat means to destroy, ruin, batter or mar.

Isaiah 52:14 As many were astonied at thee, his visage was so marred more than any man, and his form more than the sons of men:

He was beaten for hours with a Roman flagrum no more than 39 times until his flesh was falling away from his body (slain). His beard was plucked out, they placed a crown of thorns on his head, and finally, he was beaten, battered and hammered "upright" to the tree or cross. They beat him so bad that He could not be recognized. His flesh was flayed (opened) because of the flagrum (whip) that they used to beat Him. His head was bleeding because they pulled out his beard and platted a crown of long "thorns" on his head. He was crowned emblematically a king over sin because He took on the curse of mankind's sin that occurred in the garden.

Genesis 3:17 And unto Adam he said, Because thou hast hearkened unto the voice of thy wife, and hast has eaten of the tree, of which I commanded thee, saying, Thou shalt not eat of it: cursed is the ground for thy sake; in sorrow shalt thou eat of it all the days of thy *life; 18. **Thorns** also and thistles shall it bring forth to thee, and thou shalt eat the herb of the field;*

He was killed at twilight which was the prescribed time that was given in the instructions of Moses. Historically, the High Priest hollered out "It is finished" after he offered the last lamb as a sacrifice. Yahshua used that same phrase as a High Priest used, "It is finished" and He gave up the ghost!

We read in Gen.1:14 that Elohim created the luminaries for signs in the heavens. It is interesting that immediately after Yahshua died, that the sun, which was created on the fourth day, refused to give its light. A period of darkness that swept over the earth. Light briefly left the earth because they tried to put out the light of Yahshua. This was a remarkable sign to those who have insight.

John 1:5 And the light shineth in darkness and the darkness comprehended it not. (tried to put out the light)

Luke 23:44 And it was about the sixth hour, and there was a darkness over all the earth until the ninth hour. 45. And the sun was darkened, and the veil of the temple was rent in the midst. 46. And when Jesus had cried with a loud voice, he said, Father, into thy hands I commend my spirit: and having said thus, he gave up the ghost.

The death of Yahshua was the culmination of many prophecies. To some, it was received with great anticipation. However, most people were clue less about what was taking place. Even some of the disciples (talmideem) were not keenly aware of the magnitude of the events that had just taken place.

The high priest, Caiaphas received divine revelation from Elohim when questioned whether to leave Yahshua alone and risk all men believing on Him said the following;

John 11:50 Nor consider that it is expedient for us, that one man should die for the people, and that the whole nation perish not. 51. And this spake he not of himself: but being the high priest that year, he prophesied that Yahshua should die for that nation. 52. And not for that nation only, but that also He should gather together in one the children of Elohim (God) that were scattered abroad. The following are scriptural keys for studying:

Passover Keys

Old Testament	New Testament
Ex. 12:3 On the tent of this month	John 12:1 Then six days before Passover
	John 12:12 The next day…
	Matt. 21:5 King is coming to you, lowly….
Ex. 12:3 Every man take a Lamb	John 1:29 Behold the lamb of God….
	Rev. 5:6 A lamb as though it was slain…
Ex. 12:3 A lamb for a household	Matt. 21:12 My house a house of prayer
	Mark 11:11 and Luke 19:45
Ex. 12:5 Lamb without blemish	1Pet. 2:22 Who committed no sin
	2Cor.5:21 He knew no sin
	John 19:6 Find no fault in him
Ex. 12:5 A male of the first year	Mat. 1:21 Virgin shall be with child

Old Testament	New Testament
	John 3:16 Only-begotten Son
	Luke 1:31 Bring forth a son
Ex. 12:6 Keep it until the 14th day	Luke 22:1 Called Passover
	Luke 22:7 Passover must be killed
	Mark 14:1 After two days Passover
Ex. 12:6 Whole assembly kill it	John 19:14-15 Crucify Him
	Luke 23:1-2 The whole multitude
Isa. 53:5 He bore our grief	1Pet. 2:24 Bare our sins in his body
Zech 12:10 Look upon me whom they pierced	John 19:34 Soldier…pierced His side
Exo. 12:22 Take a bunch of hyssops	John 19:29 Put *it* upon hyssop
Gen 3:18 Thorns also and thistles shall it bring	John 19:5 Wearing the crown of thorns
Gen. 3:7 They sewed fig leaves together	Mk. 11:14,21 Fig tree which thou cursedst
Ex. 12:13 When I see the blood	Lk. 22:20 New Testament in my blood

Chapter Twelve: Understanding Unleavened Bread

Leviticus 23:6 And on the fifteenth day of the same month is the feast of unleavened bread unto the LORD: seven days ye must eat unleavened bread. 7. In the first day, ye shall have a holy convocation: ye shall do no servile work therein. 8. But ye shall offer an offering made by fire unto the LORD seven days: in the seventh day is a holy convocation: ye shall do no servile work therein.

We have shown many scriptures that prove that Passover was about the death of Yahshua. His death was prophesied to occur on a specific day, at a certain time and in a prearranged fashion.

What if we can show you that the second Feast of Yahweh called Unleavened Bread was specifically about His burial. The Feast of Passover was very intriguing. Now let's begin the discussion on Unleavened Bread.

The Hebrew name for the Feast of Unleavened Bread is "Chag Matzot." The 15th day of the month of Abib is the Feast of Unleavened Bread.

As discussed, prior, on the 14th and 15th day of the Biblical lunar month, there is a full moon. We should also note that the Hebrew day begins in the evening and goes from evening to evening.

Leviticus 23:6 And on the fifteenth day of the same month is the feast of unleavened bread unto the LORD: seven days ye must eat unleavened bread. 7. In the first day, ye shall have a holy convocation: ye shall do no servile work therein. 8. But ye shall offer an offering made by fire unto the LORD seven days: in the seventh day is a holy convocation: ye shall do no servile work therein.

Unleavened Bread begins immediately after Passover at 6:01 pm. This begins a new day which is the 15th of Abib. This day is treated like a Sabbath by not performing servile work. On this night, the people were instructed to eat unleavened bread, the Passover lamb, and bitter herbs.

Elohim (God) gave Moses precise instructions on how to prepare and eat the meal including the Passover Lamb. The meal is called the "Seder" meal. Seder in Hebrew means order. These are the instructions for the Seder meal:

1. They must eat the lamb on the night of the 15th which began in the evening following Passover
2. The lamb must be roasted with fire.
3. The lamb must be eaten along with unleavened bread. (matzah)
4. They had to eat the flesh along with bitter herbs.
5. They must roast all the lamb's parts. (head, legs, and insides)
6. The Israelites must gird their loins.
7. They must have shoes on their feet.
8. They must have their staff in their hand.
9. They could not eat it raw
10. They could not eat it sodden with water.
11. They could not let any of it remain until morning.
12. If anything remains, burn it with fire

Today this same meal is called the Seder meal or Passover meal. Seder means order and order is an accurate arrangement of all things. Biblically, the main elements of the meal consisted of lamb, unleavened bread (matzah) and bitter herbs.

Many European Jews add other elements such as a boiled egg and charoset (apple mixture). Who was it that added those items to a Sedar plate? It is said that the origin of the addition of the egg occurred after the Babylonian captivity. No matter whether it is true or not, neither of the elements are Biblically required.

Many people are also concerned about the other meal items. Whether we will have rice or chicken, salad or corn. This meal is unlike your daily meal. Technically, the only items necessary are the three elements we mentioned.

Paul the writer of many books in the New Testament attempted to explain the "Seder meal" to the people in 1Cor. 11:20-28:

1 Corinthians 11:20 When ye come together therefore into one place, this is not to eat the Lord's supper. 21. For in eating everyone taketh before other his own supper: and one is hungry, and another is drunken. 22. What? have ye not houses to eat and to drink in? or despise ye the church of God, and shame them that have not? What shall I say to you? shall I praise you in this? I praise you not

23. For I have received of the Lord that which also I delivered unto you, That the Lord Jesus the same night in which he was betrayed took bread: 24. And when he had given thanks, he brake it, and said, Take, eat: this is my body, which is broken for you: this do in remembrance of me. 25. After the same manner also he took the cup, when he had supped, saying, this cup is the new testament in my blood: this do ye, as oft as ye drink it, in remembrance of me.26. For as often as ye eat this bread, and drink this cup, ye do shew the Lord's death till he come.

27. Wherefore whosoever shall eat this bread, and drink this cup of the Lord, unworthily, shall be guilty of the body and blood of the Lord. 28. But let a man examine himself, and so let him eat of that bread, and drink of that cup. 29. For he that eateth and drinketh unworthily, eateth and drinketh damnation to himself, not discerning the Lord's body. 30. For this cause many are weak and sickly among you, and many sleep.

31. For if we would judge ourselves, we should not be judged. 32. But when we are judged, we are chastened of the Lord, that we should not be condemned with the world. 33. Wherefore, my brethren, when ye come together to eat, tarry one for another. 34. And if any man hunger, let him eat at home; that ye come not together unto condemnation. And the rest will I set in order when I come.

Let's be clear, the meal that Paul is referring to is the "Seder meal." Most Christians have been taught that Paul was giving instructions concerning the taking of "Communion." Absolutely not! He was teaching them about how to spiritually approach the "Seder meal."

According to the scripture in 1Corinthians 11, it is obvious people were complaining about the food they were eating. Also, some of them must have been drinking too much. They appeared to be using this meal as a time of celebration. This meal is not about how much you can eat or drink.

The "Seder" is a meal in honor of the ultimate sacrifice that Yahshua made in accordance with the instructions given by Moses. This is an ancient command that was specified in the first sentence of the Hebrew Bible. YHWH commanded this to happen from the beginning of time.

The Seder was not established as a common meal! Paul suggests that if we approach the "Seder" meal the wrong way, we can become sick or weakly. The Hebrew term for weak is "Strong's 7503 raphah" which means to become feeble, idle, slack and slothful. This is the negative end of the spectrum of the word "raphah" which means to heal.

We become slothful and idle because we do not understand the ultimate sacrifice that Yahshua gave. His body and blood became the currency for the deliverance from sin and bondage. Sin is defined as the violation of Torah.

The instructions were also specified by Moses in Exodus chapter 12. YHWH detailed the time, day, hour, type of food, and even how to eat the meal. He even declared that this was an everlasting memorial never to be done away with.

Exodus 12:8 And they shall eat the flesh in that night, roast with fire, and unleavened bread; and with bitter herbs, they shall eat it. 9. Eat not of it raw, nor sodden at all with water, but roast with fire; his head with his legs, and with the purtenance thereof. 10. And ye shall let nothing of it remain until the morning; and that which remaineth of it until the morning ye shall burn with fire.

11. And thus shall ye eat it; with your loins girded, your shoes on your feet, and your staff in your hand; and ye shall eat it in haste: it is the Lord's Passover. 12. For I will pass through the land of Egypt this night and will smite all the firstborn in the land of Egypt, both man and beast; and against all the gods of Egypt I will execute judgment: I am the LORD. 13. And the blood shall be to you for a token upon the houses where ye are: and when I see the blood, I will pass over you, and the plague shall not be upon you to destroy you when I smite the land of Egypt. 14. And this day shall be unto you for a memorial, and ye shall keep it a feast to the LORD throughout your generations; ye shall keep it a feast by an ordinance forever. 15. Seven days shall ye eat unleavened bread; even the first day ye shall put away leaven out of your houses: for whosoever eateth leavened bread from the first day until the seventh day, that soul shall be cut off from Israel.

Barley Bread:
Barley was the first grain to ripen and symbolized spring. Bread was a central focus of the Hebrew diet. During Unleavened Bread they were instructed to make flour from the barley, add water, knead it into dough and bake it in the fire.

Bread (lechem) without leaven was called "matzah." Bread (lechem) which includes yeast or leaven was called "hametz." To many Hebrews, no meal was complete without bread (lechem). *Ellen Frankel and Betsy Platkin Teutsch (1992) The Encyclopedia of Jewish Symbols, (pp24)*

The main focus on the Feast of Unleavened Bread is the unleavened bread. The bread was baked flat because of the absence of yeast. Barley was exceptional because it had a hard shell which protected it from insects and remained edible.

The baked bread is pierced and striped with what appears to be grill marks. At some point during the Seder meal, we give the participants three pieces of Matzah (unleavened bread). The leader of the table takes the middle piece of pierced and striped bread, breaks it and wraps the most significant portion in linen to be hidden away until the end of the meal.

The custom was to hide the wrapped middle piece. The middle piece is called the "Afikomen" which is a Hebrew word meaning, desert. This piece is stored away until the end of the meal. The children are then instructed to find the find the Afikomen. Sometimes they are given a reward which indicates, if we seek His face and turn from our wicked ways, our reward will be the <u>forgiveness</u> of sins.

No one truly knows the origin of these traditions, but without a doubt, they have many Messianic overtones. The name of barley (seh orah) is quite impressive. Let us separate the word "seh orah" into two words. The Hebrew word "seh" is the word for lamb. The Hebrew word "orah" means light. It is the root of the word Torah. The word when separated could mean "Lamb of the Torah." I find this to be striking and remarkable! The Torah was also called, "a lamp unto my feet and a light unto my path." Psalm 119:105.

NUN. Thy word is a lamp unto my feet, and a light unto my path.
Later, the writer John explains the concept of the expression,
"word." He also illustrates that the "word" became flesh and
lived among us.

John 1:1, In the beginning was the Word, and the Word was with
God, and the Word was God.

John 1:14 And the Word was made flesh, and dwelt among us, (and
we beheld his glory, the glory as of the only begotten of the Father,)
full of grace and truth.

Suffice it to say that if the Torah was the word, then
Yahshua was the essence of the Torah.

The Hebrew word for "grain" (barley) also refer to Yahshua the
Mashiach. The Bible in its opening verse hinted at this. The first
two letters of the Hebrew Bible begin with a "bet and resh."
(B'reshit)

When the letters, "Beit and Resh" are combined, they spell
"bar" which means grain or son. These are the first two letters
written in the Bible. You are probably wondering, "What
does that have to do with anything?" Elohim directed Moses
to begin the Bible with two letters that together spell a word
which means grain. The grain that he was referring to, most
likely could be ground into Unleavened Bread.

The word "bar" also means <u>son</u>. Why would Elohim mention
the word, son in the first two letters of Genesis? Later in the
Bible, John referred to Yahshua as the only begotten <u>son</u>. The
letters that comprise the word "bar" was coded. The Creator

intended to reveal the concept of "son and grain" within the opening of this Great Book. You can't see this if you read it in English. This was written in the heavenly language, called Hebrew. Every Hebrew letter has a name, number, sound and meaning. It is clear that the writers, Isaiah and John broke the code and wrote that Yahshua was the only begotten son. How did John make that connection?

John 3:16 For God so loved the world, that he gave his only begotten Son, that whosoever believeth in him should not perish, but have everlasting life.

Isaiah 9:6 For unto us a child is born, unto us a son is given: and the government shall be upon his shoulder: and his name shall be called Wonderful, Counsellor, The mighty God, The everlasting Father, The Prince of Peace.

Another striking Messianic reference is the fact that the matzah (unleavened bread) had stripes from the baking process. How can this tradition be so completely aligned to Yahshua and the abuse that he endured?

Isaiah 53:4 He is despised and rejected of men; a man of sorrows and acquainted with grief: and we hid as it were our faces from him; he was despised, and we esteemed him not 5. Surely, he hath borne our griefs, and carried our sorrows: yet we did esteem him stricken, smitten of God, and afflicted. 6. But he was wounded for our transgressions, he was bruised for our iniquities: the chastisement of our peace was upon him, and with his stripes, we are healed.

John 6:32 Then Jesus said unto them, Verily, verily, I say unto you, Moses gave you not that bread from heaven; but my Father giveth you the true bread from heaven. 33. For the bread of God is he which cometh down from heaven, and giveth life unto the world. 34. Then said they unto him, Lord, evermore give us this bread. 35. And Jesus said unto them, I am the bread of life: he that cometh to me shall never hunger; and he that believeth on me shall never thirst.

John 19:1 Then Pilate, therefore, took Jesus and scourged him.

The Hebrew language is more specific than the English or Greek. It is, therefore, pragmatic that two letters can provide deeper insight in the writings of the Bible than several chapters written in Greek or English. Many things were concealed from the readers of the Bible because of that translations.

Another agricultural grain spoken of in the Bible is wheat. The Hebrew term for wheat is (chittah). The harvesting of wheat occurs in late spring early summer. Unlike wheat, barley was the first grain to ripen and was used to make the "unleavened bread." The wheat grain "chittah" can be used with yeast that will cause the bread to rise or become puffy.

The Hebrew word "chittah" has the same root letters as the word "chattah." The Hebrew word "Chattah" is translated to mean "sin." Sin is defined as the "violation of Torah. So, if leaven symbolizes sin, then it could be said that the "unleavened bread" symbolized the absence of sin.

The yeast or leavening agent used in the wheat bread causes it to rise. This is an example of how sin affects you. There are three elements of sin, lust of the flesh, eye and pride of life. Pride is the type of sin that puffs you up. You start to think of yourself more highly than you ought. Pride cripples people because it causes strife, distrust and jealousy.

We have shown that the Hebrew name for barley seh orah can mean "Lamb of Torah," and the Torah represents the word of Elohim. The "Lamb of Torah" who became flesh, was crucified. He was tortured so brutally with 39 stripes, that His skin tore from his flesh. They made Him look like the "striped unleavened bread."

Just like Yahshua, the matzah is also pierced in the baking process. Examine the "matzah," and you will notice the tiny holes in it. Not many people notice the piercing on the matzah. Without a doubt, the holes are a "Messianic" reference to remind us that Yahshua was pierced in his hands, feet and side.

The following scriptures were written long before the birth of Yahushua. These scriptures describe a man that had his hand and feet pierced while He hung on a wooden object. Finally, John recorded the event using the following scriptures.

Psalms 22:16 For dogs have compassed me: the assembly of the wicked have enclosed me: they pierced my hands and my feet. 17. I may tell all my bones: they look and stare upon me. 18. They part my garments among them and cast lots upon my vesture.

Zech. 12:10 And I will pour upon the house of David, and upon the inhabitants of Jerusalem, the spirit of grace and supplications: and they shall look upon me whom they have pierced, and they shall mourn for him, as one mourneth for his only son, and shall be in bitterness for him, as one that is in agony for his firstborn.

John 19:34 But one of the soldiers with a spear pierced his side, and forthwith came there out blood and water.

The "Afikomen" is the most amazing tradition that has been kept by the Hebrew community for thousands of years. During the "Seder" meal, each table is given three pieces of matzah. The middle portion is called the Afikomen.

We ask the leader of the table to take the middle piece and break it. Once the middle piece is broken, it is wrapped in linen and stored away until the end of the meal. This is a depiction of the burial of Yahushua. Note the following scriptures;

Luke 23:32 And there were also two others, malefactors, led with him to be put to death. 33. And when they came to the place, which is called Calvary, there they crucified him, and the malefactors, one on the right hand, and the other on the left. 34. Then said Jesus, Father, forgive them; for they know not what they do. And they parted his raiment and cast lots.

Mark 15:27 And with him they crucify two thieves; the one on his right hand, and the other on his left.

Mark 15:43 Joseph of Arimathaea, an honorable counselor, which also waited for the kingdom of God, came, and went in boldly unto Pilate, and craved the body of Jesus. 44. And Pilate marveled if he were already dead: and calling unto him the centurion, he asked him whether he had been any while dead. 45. And when he knew it of the centurion, he gave the body to Joseph. 46. And he bought fine linen, and took him down, and wrapped him in the linen, and laid him in a sepulcher which was hewn out of a rock and rolled a stone unto the door of the sepulcher.

We know that you are convinced that the "Feast of Unleavened Bread" refers to the burial of Yahushua. These customs and traditions aren't mindless rituals; they are types and shadows of the actual events that took place in Yahshua's life.

We now know about the rituals, customs, and traditions as it relates to the "Seder" meal. However, what about the first "Feast of Unleavened Bread?" How does the first feast during the time of Moses, relate to a burial? It is apparent that more "sod," exegesis, and digging is necessary. I went back to the 12th chapter of the Book of Exodus to find the answer.

During the first "Seder" meal the Egyptians were experiencing the death of the firstborn of men and beasts throughout all the land. There was great anguish, and mourning heard everywhere. However, the Hebrews were safe on the other side of the blood except for those that did not heed the instructions of Moses. After the meal, Moses called for Aaron and the leaders to rise because it was time to go.

Exodus 12:31 And Pharaoh rose up in the night, he, and all his servants, and all the Egyptians; and there was a great cry in Egypt; for there was not a house where there was not one dead. 32. Also take your flocks and your herds, as ye have said, and be gone; and bless me also. 33. And the Egyptians were urgent upon the people, that they might send them out of the land in haste; for they said, we (Ebonics) be all dead men.

34. And the people took their dough before it was leavened, their kneading troughs being bound up in their clothes upon their shoulders. 35. And the children of Israel did according to the word of Moses, and they borrowed of the Egyptians jewels of silver, and jewels of gold, and raiment: 36. And the LORD gave the people favor in the sight of the Egyptians so that they lent unto them such things as they required. And they spoiled the Egyptians.

Exodus 13:4 This day came ye out in the month Abib.

The Children of Israel were obedient, rose up and journeyed to the Red Sea. Moses took the bones of Joseph with him as was promised. Yahweh went before them in a pillar of cloud by day and fire by night. The Egyptian's Pharaoh hardened his heart and began a nationwide hunt. The Egyptians came upon the Hebrew at the Red Sea. The Israelites were loaded with cattle, children, gold and silver, and many other articles but had nowhere to go. The Egyptians were behind them and the sea before them. The Elohim (God) instructed Moses to stretch out his staff in his hand, and the sea parted, and the ground became dry so they could cross. Note the following scriptures;

Exodus 14:26 And the LORD said unto Moses, stretch out thine hand over the sea, that the waters may come again upon the Egyptians, upon their chariots, and upon their horsemen. 27. And Moses stretched forth his hand over the sea, and the sea returned to his strength when the morning appeared, and the Egyptians fled against it, and the LORD overthrew the Egyptians in the midst of the sea.

28. And the waters returned and covered the chariots, and the horsemen, and all the host of Pharaoh that came into the sea after them; there remained not so much as one of them. 29. But the children of Israel walked upon dry land in the midst of the sea, and the waters were a wall unto them on their right hand, and on their left.

The Children of Israel were amidst the sea, surrounded by water. Today, we call this baptism. A baptism is a form of burial by water. I will refer back to the beginning of the Bible so that we can get a better understanding.

Gen. 1:6 And God said, let there be a firmament in the midst of the waters, and let it divide the waters from the waters.

In that verse, the word firmament (Strong's 7549 riqiyah) means to expand or expanse, the visible arch of the sky, spread abroad. The Elohim (God) divided or separated (Strong's 910 bidad) the waters from the waters. The sky or firmament is made up of water that was separated from the water beneath. Moses parted the sea leaving walls of water on both sides of them and water was also above. The children of Israel were baptized in the water. They were immersed in the depths of the sea and had walls of water on each side and water above. The term which means submerge in the Hebrew language is (Strong's 2881 tabal, tabalah) to dip, plunge. There is also a

Hebrew term which the New Testament (Brit Hadashah) word baptism derived and that word is from (Strong's 4724 mikvehs) which means a collection of water.

The word references ceremonial cleansing. A person who was considered impure or ritually unclean was immersed in a mikveh. The immersion in water changed the status of the person from unclean to ceremonially clean. This must be done, in order to enter the Temple.

There were several reasons why a person could be considered unclean or impure;
1. Men who had a discharge
2. Women who just gave birth
3. One who comes in contact with a dead body
4. A woman on a monthly cycle

Any natural body of water collected below the ground could be considered a mikveh. A swimming pool is not considered a mikveh because it does not have natural running water. A lake is regarded as a great mikveh because it is all natural and flowing.

Lev. 15:19 And if a woman has an issue, and her issue in her flesh be blood, she shall be put apart seven days: and whosoever toucheth her shall be unclean until the even.

Lev. 11:36 Nevertheless a fountain or pit, wherein there is plenty of water, shall be clean: but that which toucheth their carcass shall be unclean.

1 Cor. 10:1 Moreover, brethren, I would not that ye should be ignorant, how that all our fathers were under the cloud, and all passed through the sea; 2. And were all baptized unto Moses in the cloud and in the sea; 3. And did all eat the same spiritual meat; 4.

And did all drink the same spiritual drink: for they drank of that spiritual Rock that followed them: and that Rock was Christ.

Romans 6:5 Know ye not, that so many of us as were baptized into Jesus Christ were baptized into his death? 6. Therefore we are buried with him by baptism into death: that like as Christ was raised up from the dead by the glory of the Father, even so, we also should walk in newness of life.

Moshe and the Children of Israel were submerged into the parted dry sea, with water on both sides and water above. This experience is considered a ritual cleansing mikveh or baptism. The writer Paul described it in 1 Corinthians 10;

1 Corinthians 10:1 Moreover, brethren, I would not that ye should be ignorant, how that all our fathers were under the cloud, and all passed through the sea; 2. And were all baptized unto Moses in the cloud and in the sea;

This immersion ritual became one of the leading practices used by the Christians to symbolize a person's movement from sinner to saint or unclean to clean. Water represented a status change. When you are submerged in the mikveh or baptism, you are considered ritually dead to sin and your status changes from sinner to believer.

This term (mikveh) also comes from the root word (Strong's 6960 Qavah, to expect, patiently, wait, tarry). Once you have completed your mikveh, you remain or tarry for your spiritual or ritual change.

Ex. 12:39 And they baked unleavened cakes of the dough which they brought forth out of Egypt, for it was not leavened; because they were thrust out of Egypt, and could not tarry, neither had they prepared for themselves any victual.

Luke 24:49 And, behold, I send the promise of my Father upon you: but tarry ye in the city of Jerusalem, until ye be endued with power from on high.

So far, we have drawn the correlation between Passover and the "death" of the lamb and firstborn. The theme of the Feast of Unleavened Bread is that of a "burial.' The Children of Israel were baptized by passing through the sea. The sea was considered a watery grave. After Yahshua "gave up the ghost," He was taken down from the stake, by Joseph. They <u>wrapped him in linen and placed him in a tomb</u> (grave) that no man had ever been. During the Seder meal, we take the middle of the three matzah pieces, break it, <u>wrap it in linen and hide it away.</u>

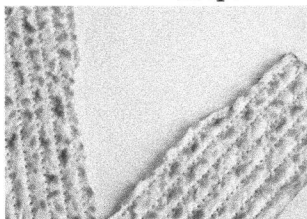

Unleavened Bread Keys

Old Testament	New Testament
Lev. 23:6 Eat unleavened bread	Lk. 22:19 He took bread and gave thanks
Ex. 12:8 eat the flesh in that night	Lk. 22:15 Desired to eat this Passover
Ex. 14:22 Children of Israel went into the midst of the sea	1Cor. 10:2 Baptized unto Moses in the cloud and in the sea;
	Rom. 6:3 were baptized into his death.

Old Testament	New Testament
	Col. 2:12 Buried with him in baptism, wherein also ye have risen with *him*
Lev. 23:6 fifteenth day of the same month *is*, the feast of unleavened bread	Mk. 14:12 first day of unleavened bread

Chapter Thirteen: Feast of Firstfruits

The third feast day is the "Feast of Firstfruits." If this feast follows the same logical pattern, it should represent "redemption and resurrection."

On the day after the weekly Sabbath during the week of Passover, begins the Feast of Firstfruits. This feast day commemorates the period that the Hebrews went down into the depths of the Red Sea as slaves and came up (resurrected) on the other side as free men and women. According to the Bible, during this Festival the priest present a sheaf of the first fruit of the barley harvest as a "gift" unto the Most High. This practice of offering the first fruit of the harvest taught the Hebrews that it was not the sower, nor the reaper which caused the bountiful harvest, only Yah. The first fruits are at the beginning of the ripened grain in the springtime. This first fruit of the grain is evidence that the entire yearly harvest is on the way.

Yahshua died on Passover. They buried Him on the Feast of Unleavened Bread. Therefore, He must have been resurrected on the Feast of Firstfruits. Let's now examine the scriptures and see.

Lev. 23:9 And the LORD spake unto Moses, saying, 10. Speak unto the children of Israel, and say unto them, when ye have come into the land which I give unto you, and shall reap the harvest thereof, then ye shall bring a sheaf of the first fruits of your harvest unto the priest: 11. Moreover, he shall wave the sheaf before the LORD, to be accepted for you: on the morrow after the sabbath the priest shall wave it. 12. And ye shall offer that day when ye wave the sheaf he lamb without blemish of the first year for a burnt offering unto the LORD. 13. And the meat offering thereof shall be two tenth deals of fine flour mingled with oil, an offering made by fire unto the LORD for a sweet savor: and the drink offering thereof shall be of wine, the fourth part of an hin.14. And ye shall eat neither bread, nor parched corn, nor green ears, until the selfsame day that ye have brought an offering unto your God: it shall be a statute forever throughout your generations in all your dwellings.

There is much controversy concerning the Biblical date of the Feast of First Fruits. Without debate, however, Good Friday is celebrated throughout the world. This concept involves the death, burial, and resurrection of Yahshua Ha Mashiach/Jesus. They set (6th day) of the week, Friday as the day to observe the crucifixion of Yahshua Ha Mashiach. The world keeps Easter as the day of His resurrection on the Sunday following.

The reason the Catholic Church set "Good Friday" in place was thought to provide consistent yearly days to observe the crucifixion and the resurrection. Every year, people gather in their churches from 12:00 to 3:00 pm on Friday before Easter to have elaborate ceremonies and worship meetings. They sometimes provide re-enactments of Yahshua on the cross or someone simulating Him carrying the cross with large crowds cheering and jeering. There is no question that these beautiful spectacles insight endearing emotions of love, sadness, and praise.

I have personally witnessed great concerts, plays and my favorite, "the living depiction of Leonardo De Vinci's painting of the Last Supper." I saw it several times in Germany, and it was one of the most outstanding events that I have ever seen. These things are all well-intentioned, beautifully executed and spiritually charged.

Despite the sincerity of the people surrounding these events, they are still participating in an act that attempts to make Yahshua out of a liar. First, we must consider that the period from 3:00 Friday to 6:00 Sunday adds up to only 39 hours. This 39-hour period is in direct contradiction to the scriptures:

Matt. 12:39 But he answered and said unto them, an evil and adulterous generation seeketh after a sign; and there shall no sign be given to it, but the sign of the prophet Jonas: 40. For as Jonas was three days and three nights in the whale's belly; so shall the Son of man be three days and three nights in the heart of the earth.

Yahshua was explicit, precise and deliberate when he described the aftermath of His crucifixion. He said that He would be in the heart of the earth for three days and three nights. According to my calculation, the period of three days and three nights totals 72 hours. I have heard many people try to explain the Friday to Sunday scenario in several ways, but the numbers never add up.

The "Friday to Sunday" crucifixion contradicts the words of the Savior. Yahshua clarified how much time is in a day and a night. He eliminated the confusion by specifying a 24-hour day. Please read Matt. 12:39-40;

John 11:9 Jesus answered, Are there not <u>twelve hours</u> in the day? If any man walks in the day, he stumbleth not, because he seeth the light of this world. 1But if a man walks in the night, he stumbleth, because there is no light in him.

Yahshua knew that daylight consisted of 12 hours. The night also consists of 12 hours. The two combined total twenty-four hours. The same thing is recorded in Genesis 1:4 ... the evening and morning were the first day. Most of you reading this will say to yourself, "what difference does it make? Yahshua answered that question in the following scriptures;

Mark 7:9 And he said unto them, Full well ye reject the

commandment of God, that ye may keep your tradition.

Mark 7:13 Making the word of God of none effect through your tradition, which ye have delivered: and many such like things do ye.

Matt. 27:63 Saying, Sir, we remember that that deceiver said, while he was yet alive, after three days I will rise again. 64. Command therefore that the sepulcher is made sure until the third day, lest his disciples come by night, and steal him away, and say unto the people, He has risen from the dead: so, the last error shall be worse than the first.

Mark 8:31 And he began to teach them, that the Son of man must suffer many things, and be rejected of the elders, and of the chief priests, and scribes, and be killed, and after three days rise again.

John 2:19 Jesus answered and said unto them, destroy this temple, and in three days I will raise it up. 20. Then said the Jews, Forty and six years was this temple in building, and wilt thou rear it up in three days? 21. But he spoke of the temple of his body

Mark 8:31, Matthew 27:63 and John2:19,21 all indicate that after three days, he would rise again. We must choose to accept the Biblical quotes from Yahshua, or should we continue to follow the traditions handed to us by the Catholic Church?

Why do modern-day Christians follow these widely accepted views that Yahshua died on the cross on a Friday and rose from the grave on a Sunday morning?
The truth is, when we keep these fictitious dates and times, we are calling Yahshua a liar. We should all pay close attention to the dates and times that Yahweh provides us. The truth that you are seeking is in the Bible hidden in plain sight. Sometimes, because of our religious orientations, we tend to

overlook scriptures that don't line up with our traditions and teachings.

If Yahshua said that He would be in the heart of the earth three days and three nights, shouldn't we find this information in the Bible?

Before we move on, I must deal with one more problematic issue, and that is the use of the word "Easter" to describe an event associated with my Savior's resurrection. It is appalling to know that the Catholic Church deliberately named the event attached to our salvation and His resurrection after a pagan goddess. I will use the secular dictionaries and encyclopedias to prove this point.

According to (the American College Dictionary, C.L. Barnhart, Jess Stein, Random House) the definition of Easter is 1) An annual Christian festival in commemoration of the resurrection of Jesus Christ, observed on the first Sunday after the "full moon" that occurs on or next after March 21. 2) The day on which this festival is celebrated. (ME ester, OE eastre, pl. eastron, c. G Ostern, pl.) orig. name of a goddess; akin to aurora dawn, Gk eos cf. East. Aurora, ...1) Class myth. Dawn often personified by the Romans and others as a goddess (Eos). 2) The rise of the dawn of something.

(A Dictionary of the Bible, Royal Publishers, Inc. pp. 193) Originally the spring festival in honor of Eastra or Ostara, the Teutonic goddess of light and spring. As early as the eighth century, the name was transferred by the Anglo-Saxons to the Christian festival designed to celebrate the resurrection of Christ. In the A.V. it occurs once, viz., Acts 12:4, but is a mistranslation. The original is Pascha, the ordinary Greek word for Passover. The R.V. properly employs the word Passover.

(The World Book Encyclopedia, Copyright 1985, USA) the Easter festival is closely associated with spring. The new plant life that

appears in spring symbolizes the new life Christians gain because for Jesus Crucifixion and Resurrection. The word Easter may have come from an early English word, Eastre. Some scholars say Eastre was the name of a pagan goddess of spring, the name of a Spring festival, or the name of the season itself.

(The Two Babylons, PP.103 by Alexander Hislop) states, it bears the Chaldean origin on its forehead. Easter is nothing else than Astarte, one of the titles of Beltis, Queen of Heaven.

(Austen H. Layard, Nineveh, and Babylon, Vol. II pp. 629) The ancient gods of the pagans had many different names. While this goddess was called Astarte by the Phoenicians, it appears on the Assyrian monuments found by Layard in excavations at Nineveh as Ishtar.

(The New American Bible, Catholic Bible Publishers, pp. 101) "The Queen of Heaven" 1. Popular title for the Blessed Virgin, in litanies and prayers.

(The Old Testament of The Jerusalem Bible Copyright 1966 by Darton, Longman & Todd, Ltd. And Doubleday & Company, Inc. pp 1264, 1319) Jer. 7:18 The children collect the wood, the fathers light the fire, the women knead the dough, to make cakes for the Queen of Heaven; and, to spite me, they pour libations to alien gods that they might provoke me to anger.

Jer. 44:16-18 We have no intention of listening to this word you have spoken to us in Yahweh's name, but intend to go on doing all we have vowed to do: offering incense to the Queen of Heaven and pouring libations in her honor, as we used to do, we and our fathers, our kings and our leaders, in the towns of Judah and in the streets of Jerusalem: we had food in plenty then, we lived well, we suffered no disasters. But since we gave up offering incense to the Queen of Heaven and pouring libations in her honor, we have been destitute and have perished either by sword or by famine.

We have sighted several different sources which all substantiate the fact that the term "Easter" is pagan. We also know that the etymology of Easter dates back to the pagan goddess Ishtar. How can we not know this? We live in the information age. If you want to know something, all you have to do is "google" a subject on your mobile phone, and it comes right up. We are without excuse!

Lent:
You can't have a serious discussion about Easter without first discussing the practice called "Lent." The Pagan priests were astrologers who closely monitored the positions of the sun, moon, 5 of the planets and constellations of stars. These were the physical deities they worshipped.

They calculated times of the year based on sex. They knew the path of the sun crossed the celestial equator at the vernal (spring) and autumnal equinoxes producing equal days and nights at those events.

The festival of Easter involved the "Rites of Spring" near the Equinox of Venus when pagans believed the Earth Mother was impregnated by the sun. They engaged in ritual sex acts and used symbols of fertility like eggs, rabbits, and hot cross buns.

Lent is the practice and custom of fasting for 40 days before Easter. It is most prevalent among those that are of the Catholic orientation. However, many Protestant congregants use this practice thinking that it spiritually brings them closer to Yahshua (Jesus) by denying their desire to eat certain foods. Many people are sincere and are innocently unaware of its Pagan origins.

Many such 40-day fasts existed long before the Catholic Church. They copied the forty days for Lent from the worshippers of the Babylonian goddess. Such a Lent of forty days, "in the spring of the year," is still observed by the Yezidis or Pagan Devil-worshippers of Koordistan, who inherited it from their early masters, the Babylonians.

"Three days after the vernal (spring) equinox began the solemn fast of forty days in honor of the sun." Such a Lent of forty days was observed in Egypt.
"Wilkinson's Egyptian Antiquities, vol.1. p. 278." The Two Babylons, Alexander Hyslop, pp 105.

The Babylonian symbol for the female was and is, a circle with a crux (cross). They eat round cakes during the season of Lent as a tribute to the "Queen of Heaven or the Great Mother."

Jer. 44:18 But since we left off to burn incense to the queen of heaven, and to pour out drink offerings unto her, we have wanted all things, and have been consumed by the sword and by the famine. 19. And when we burned incense to the queen of heaven and poured out drink offerings unto her, did we make her cakes to worship her, and pour out drink offerings unto her, without our men?

In some societies, they call these cakes "bouns or buns." The buns are made of fine flour and honey. Even though these hot cross buns are not offered anymore to the "Queen of Heaven,"

we still eat them today. The "bouns" we eat today, are identical to the cake worship that was used in Athens 1500 years before the Christian era as in the days of Cecropia, the founder of Athens.
"Wilkinson's Egyptian Antiquities, vol.1. p. 278." The Two Babylons, Alexander Hyslop, pp 105.

In Babylonian mythology, Nimrod took his mother, Semiramis as his wife. At his death, his wife/mother consoled the people of Sumer by saying she carried Nimrod's child and named him Tammuz. Nimrod she explained, had gone into the heavens and was now the sun! So, the sun became the "father" and the Earth was now the "mother." She became worshipped as Ishtar which is the same word that we have today in "Easter." Nimrod's mother is called by many names, around the world such as Asherah, Ashtoreth, Ishtar, Eostre, Astarte, Maia, Gaia, Diana, Ninurta, Nana, Ceres, Ostara, Austron, Isis/Nut, Aphrodite, Venus, Insrani, Devaki, Cybele, Artemis, and Athena.

Nimrod became worshipped as Moloch, Baal, Mithras and many more. We also know that Baal disguises himself as a female such as Ishtar. Images of Ishtar can be seen depicted wearing seven horns like that of Lady Liberty in the New York harbor.

Easter was a pagan spring observance brought into Catholicism by Constantine I at Nicaea in 325 CE. Constantine re-invented the meaning behind Easter in order to abandon the Hebrew festival of Passover. He also, established the practice of Sunday, possibly to supersede the Biblical scriptural day of rest.

The Egg:
The egg is presently the most potent symbol for Easter in most countries around the world. Many Christians ignore its pagan origin or embrace it by saying it represents Jesus birth into the world protected by the shell.

The classic poet is full of the fable of the mystic egg of the Babylonians; and thus its tale is told by Hyginus, the Egyptian, the learned keeper of the Palatine library at Rome, in the time of Augustus, who was skilled in all the wisdom of his native country: "An egg of wondrous size is said to have fallen from heaven into the river Euphrates.

The fishes rolled it to the bank, where the doves having settled upon it and hatched it, out came Ishtar, who afterward was called the Syrian Goddess, Astarte. The Two Babylons, The Papal Worship, Rev. Alexander Hyslop, pp. 109, A & B Publishers Group, Brooklyn New York,

The Feast of Firstfruits:
Lev. 23:9 And the LORD spake unto Moses, saying, 10. Speak unto the children of Israel, and say unto them, When ye be come into the land which I give unto you and shall reap the harvest thereof, then ye shall bring a sheaf of the first fruits of your harvest unto the priest: 11. And he shall wave the sheaf before the LORD, to be accepted for you: on the morrow after the sabbath the priest shall wave it. 12. And ye shall offer that day when ye wave the sheaf an he lamb without blemish of the first year for a burnt offering unto the LORD. 13. And the meat offering thereof shall be two tenth deals of fine flour mingled with oil, an offering made by fire unto the LORD for a sweet savor: and the drink offering thereof shall be of wine, the fourth part of a hin. 14. And ye shall eat neither bread, nor parched corn, nor green ears, until the selfsame day that ye have brought an offering unto your God: it shall be a statute forever throughout your generations in all your dwellings.

The first Hebrew experience of the Feast of Firstfruits occurred immediately after the Feast of Unleavened Bread when they went into the depths of the Red Sea, water on both sides and a pillar of cloud during the day. Water completely surrounded them. Their descent in to the dry land/sea was like being at the bottom of a watery grave. The went down into the sea, captives, and slaves to the Egyptians. When they exited on the other side, they were a free nation of people. All this happened on the Feast of Firstfruits. In a sense, they became resurrected from death to freedom.

Let's examine the word first fruit. Two Hebrew/Eber words describe the term First Fruits. We found the first word in the book of Lev. 2.

Lev. 2:14 And if thou offer a meat offering of thy firstfruits unto the LORD, thou shalt offer for the meat offering of thy firstfruits green ears of corn dried by the fire, even corn beaten out of full ears.

The term used here is the Hebrew word (Bikkurim). This word comes from the root (Bakar) which means the first fruit to ripen, hasty fruit or (bekor) the firstborn. It also means a promise to come. Similiar to the Hebrew word (Ayin Tav), insight into the covenant cross, this word refers to a future sign.

You can find the principle of first fruits throughout the Bible. It deals with all the things that are "first." The first fruits are the first crop that belongs to God. This first crop usually governs the rest of the fruit to follow or becomes the promised fruit of what is to come. Firstfruits establish the law of first things in your life. Scholars believed that If the first of the things you receive is good or Tamim, the balance should be as good or better (Tamim.)

If the term "bikurim" meant the first to ripen, this term comes from the Hebrew/Eber word "bekor" which also means the first born or promise to come. We can, therefore, say that first fruits refer to the promise of the firstborn.

The second Hebrew/Eber word for first fruits is the word

"reshyth." It means the first in place, in time, order or rank, beginning, summit, the chief or the ruler. This word describes a position and a person. It is interesting that the first Hebrew/Eber word in the Bible has the word reshyth in it.

It reads, Bereshyth bara Elohim ET HaShamayim VaET HaEretz. בְּרֵאשִׁית בָּרָא אֱלֹהִים אֵת הַשָּׁמַיִם וְאֵת הָאָרֶץ:

Within the first word in the first sentence of our Bible, we find the word "first fruit." The first word in our Bible provides us a promise of the firstborn ruler. If you put together the shin, and resh, you will have the Hebrew word, "Sar." This word means ruler or prince, a head person of rank or class: chief, governor, lord, master, from 8323 sarar meaning to have dominion as a ruler.

Based on what we learned in the first chapter, the strong master or ruler who is the son would be nailed to the covenant cross between heaven and the earth.

The sixth Hebrew/Eber word in this first sentence in our Bible is the word VaET. This word is powerful!! The letters are;

Vav	=	Nail
Aleph	=	Strong
Tav	=	Covenant or cross

It could mean, "nailing the strong covenant to the cross." Let's take a look at another interesting observation. Please notice that the sixth word is between the fifth and the seventh words. The fifth word means "heaven," and the seventh word means "earth." When we take a closer look at it, we read, "they nailed the strong one to the cross between heaven and earth." However, the first word Reshyth referred to the resurrection of the son who was the head of the house and ruler who had dominion.

Are you surprised that all this information is in the first sentence in your Bible? Don't be alarmed, all of what we believe was planned out in detail from the beginning. The death, burial and resurrection were well planned. He started the Bible out by telling us about the plan that He eventually executed without a hitch.

When we read the Bible in the transliterated English language, we will never find any of what I just described. The reason is that the Bible was written in the Hebrew/Eber language, by Hebrews and is a Hebrew/Eber history book. It is incredible how the Hebrew/Eber language unlocks the things that are lying dormant in the English texts.

We said before that if Passover represented the death of Yahshua, and the feast of Unleavened Bread represented the burial of Yahshua, then the feast of First Fruits should represent the resurrection of Yahshua. Let's see what the scripture says;

1 Cor. 15:19 If in this life only we have hope in Christ, we are of all men most miserable. 20. But now is Christ risen from the dead and become the first fruits of them that slept. 21. For since by man came death, by man came also the resurrection of the dead.

Romans 8:22 For we know that the whole creation groaneth and travaileth in pain together until now. 23. And not only they but ourselves also, which have the first fruits of the Spirit, even we groan within ourselves, waiting for the adoption, to wit, the redemption of our body.

Good Friday:
Now, let's see what the Bible says regarding the 72-hour burial and resurrection versus the 39 hours lie called "Good Friday." We must first understand that the Hebrews followed a lunar/solar day which began at 6:01 each evening and

ended at 6:00 the following evening. We know based on history that Passover at the time that led to Yahshua's crucifixion began on Tuesday evening and ended at 6:00 Wednesday evening.

(Please review the calendar illustration.) The actual crucifixion was at noon mid-day until 3:00 afternoon on Wednesday. Sometime between 12:00 and 6:00 Joseph of Arimathea went to Pilate and asked for the body of Yahshua. At 6:01 began another lunar day, and it was the Feast of Unleavened Bread.

The Feast of Unleavened Bread is similar to the weekly Sabbath. You are not to work just like the weekly Sabbath. While Yahshua (Jesus) hung on the stake, Joseph was under time constraints because he had to get the body of Yahshua (Jesus) and bury it before 6:00. It was during this time that he wrapped the body in linen and put in a grave hewn out the mountain. Mary Magdalene and Mary, the mother of Joses, eventually saw where the body was entombed.

From Wednesday at 6:01 to Thursday 6:00 was a Feast Day Sabbath. (Shabbaton) The two Marys wanted to buy spices to anoint the body, but they could not go on Thursday during the daylight hours because it was a Sabbath and they could not buy or sell on that day. After 6:00 it was night time when it was not proper for the women to travel at night. They waited until Friday morning to go out and bought spices.

Mark 16:1 And when the sabbath was past, Mary Magdalene, and Mary the mother of James, and Salome, had bought sweet spices, that they might come and anoint him.

That same Friday during the daylight hours they returned from buying the spices and prepared the spices and fragrant oils. Friday evening at 6:01 began the weekly Sabbath. They had not completed preparing the spices and oils until later because the Bible says that they had to rest on the Sabbath according to the commandment (weekly Sabbath).

Luke 23:56 And they returned, and prepared spices and ointments, and rested the sabbath day according to the commandment.

There were two Sabbaths during that week of the Crucifixion. The first Sabbath was a Feast day Sabbath for the Feast of Unleavened Bread.

Lev. 23:6 And on the fifteenth day of the same month is the feast of unleavened bread unto the LORD: seven days ye must eat unleavened bread. 7. In the first day, ye shall have a holy convocation: ye shall do no servile work therein.

The second Sabbath was a weekly Sabbath according to the 4th commandment. Now let's do a quick review and take the time to number the days to see if Yahshua lied or did the Pope lie. Yahshua was crucified on noon Wednesday and hung for 3 hours until 3:00. Joseph took the body down, wrapped it in linen and put in an unmarked tomb at least by approximately 5:30. The two Marys followed and saw where the body was and planned to anoint the body with spices and oils. The Feast Day Sabbath of Unleavened Bread was upon them, so they rested until Friday morning. On Friday they got up went and bought the spices and came back and prepared the ointment, but the weekly Sabbath was upon them, so they rested until early 1st Day / Sunday. By the time that they got to the tomb, He was no longer there.

5:59 Wednesday	-	5:59 Thursday
24 hours		
5:59 Thursday	-	5:59 Friday
24 hours		

5:59 Friday   -   5:59 Sabbath
<u>24 hours</u>
Total
72 hours

He rose on Sabbath, shortly before the 1st day/Sunday began at 6:01. The truth is in the Bible, but it's hidden in plain sight from the wise and the prudent. The books of Mark and Luke point it out plainly but because we were oriented to believe "Good Friday" we had our eyes blinded.

The Feast of Passover represented the Death of Yahshua the Lamb of God. The Feast of Unleavened Bread represents the burial of Yahshua which we have proven lasted 72 hours just like He said and The Feast of Firstfruits was a type and shadow of His Resurrection. Join us as we explore the next feast called the Feast of Pentecost. In Hebrew/Eber language this feast is called Shavuot.

Keys for Firstfruits

Old Testament	New Testament
Lev. 23:11 On the morrow after the sabbath	John 20:1 first *day* of the week cometh Mary Magdalene early
Lev. 2:14 Offer for the meat offering of thy firstfruits בִּכּוּרִים (Bikkurim, first born) green ears	Two words for firstfruits:
Lev. 23:10 Bring a sheaf of the firstfruits (רֵאשִׁית reshit, first in time)	1Cor. 15:19 But now is Christ risen from the dead and become the firstfruits of them that slept.

Old Testament	New Testament
	Rom. 8:23 ourselves also, which have the firstfruits of the Spirit
The three-day resurrection: Mat. 12:40 For as Jonas was three days and three nights in the whale's belly; so shall the Son of man be three days and three nights in the heart of the earth.	Mk. 16:1 And when the sabbath was past, Mary Magdalene, and Mary the *mother* of James, and Salome, had bought sweet spices, that they might come and anoint him.
	Lk. 23:56 And they returned, and prepared spices and ointments, and rested the sabbath day according to the commandment.

Chapter Fourteen: Shavuot

Deut. 16:16 Three times in a year shall all thy males appear before the Lord thy God in the place which he shall choose; in the Feast of Unleavened Bread, and in the Feast of Weeks, and in the Feast of Tabernacles: and they shall not appear before the Lord empty:

Pentecost, Greek word for fifty occurred on the fiftieth day after Firstfruits. From the early 200 A.D., Christians celebrated Pentecost on the 7th Sunday (1st day) as one of their most celebrated holidays. It commemorated the descent of the Holy Spirit upon the Apostles. (Acts 2:1-4) Yahshua had promised the Holy Spirit as the comforter.

(John 14:15) If ye love me, keep my commandments.

16. And I will pray the Father, and he shall give you another Comforter, that he may abide with you forever; 17. Even the Spirit of truth; whom the world cannot receive, because it seeth him not, neither knoweth him: but ye know him; for he dwelleth with you, and shall be in you.) Pentecost was later called Whitsunday or White Sunday because newly baptized converts wore their white baptismal robes on that day.

The Hebrew word for Pentecost is Shavuot. It is the celebration of the day that the Ten Commandments were given at Mt. Sinai. (Ex. 20:1-17) The Ten Commandments were in the Ark of the Covenant along with the manna and Aaron's rod that budded during the Tabernacle and Temple times. The people on their journey carried the Ark through the wilderness as a visible reminder of the covenant and the presence of Elohim.

It is still the tradition to read the Ten Commandments during the Feast of Shavuot. They also read the Book of Ruth because of its association with the end of the barley harvest and her acceptance of the Torah just as Israel did at Mt. Sinai. There is also the theme of the "kinsman redeemer" that is pervasive throughout the reading of the book of Ruth.

The males were required to take three journeys which took place at three different times a year. The first journey took place during the season of Passover. During this time, three "Feasts" took place within one week, Passover, Unleavened Bread and the Feast of Firstfruits. The males were required to appear; however, the entire family usually made the journey. If they lived close, they even brought the animals to be used as the sacrificial offerings. However, during the time of Yahshua, they could purchase the animal once they arrived. Eventually, this led to corruption where they began selling and reselling the same animals.

Luke 19:45 And he went into the temple and began to cast out them that sold therein, and them that bought; 46. Saying unto them, it is written, My house is the house of prayer: but ye have made it a den of thieves.

The second journey took place 50 days later at the time of the wheat harvest which is called the Feast of Shavuot. The Hebrew word "Shavuot" is the plural of the word Shavua which means "week." In the English language, the Feast is called the "Feast of Weeks."

Lev. 23:15 And ye shall count unto you from the morrow after the sabbath, from the day that ye brought the sheaf of the wave offering; seven sabbaths shall be complete: 16. Even unto the morrow after the seventh sabbath shall ye number fifty days; and ye shall offer a new meat offering unto the LORD.

This particular Feast has garnered much controversy within

the Hebrew community. There are three "Feasts" that require counting the omer (Firstfruits, Shavuot and Yom Kippur). The scripture says, count from the morrow (day) after the Sabbath, seven sabbaths were to be complete. The day following the seventh sabbath was the 50th day which was the day of the celebration.

Sounds simple; however, the controversy comes from the counting to arrive at "The Feast of Firstfruits."

Lev. 23:9 And the LORD spoke unto Moses, saying, 10. Speak unto the children of Israel, and say unto them, When ye be come into the land which I give unto you and shall reap the harvest thereof, then ye shall bring a sheaf of the firstfruits of your harvest unto the priest: 11. And he shall wave the sheaf before the LORD, to be accepted for you: on the morrow after the sabbath the priest shall wave it.

What many scholars argue over is whether the "morrow after the Sabbath" is the weekly Shabbat or the Feast of Unleavened Bread. The "Feast of Unleavened Bread" is a feast day is a day of rest, the same as a Sabbath.

Many who read verse 11 in English interpret this as implying that the "Feast of Fruits" should occur the day after Unleavened Bread which would be the 16th of Abib. Passover occurs on the 14th day, Unleavened Bread the 15th day and they have interpreted Firstfruits to occur immediately following Unleavened Bread on the 16th day.

The Hebrew scriptures do not say that! The Hebrew language is concise and precise. It says what it means and means what it says. The term (Morrow, machorat, מִמָּחֳרַת) used in verse 11 indicates the next day. We agree that morrow means the following day because the Hebrew word confirms it. The question then becomes, which Sabbath? Does the counting begin on the Sabbath "Unleavened Bread" or is it the weekly Sabbath? The writer used the Hebrew words Ha Shabbat or The Sabbath after the word "machorat, morrow." It is apparent that the reference was to the weekly sabbath rather than Unleavened Bread. The Most High is very specific about dates and times, why would He be ambiguous concerning which day we are to meet? He used the term, "the Shabbat" or the weekly Sabbath is the day that the counting begins.

If the Most High wanted the counting to begin after Unleavened Bread, He would have said machorat (morrow) after Matzot (unleavened bread). Also, He was specific when stating that Passover was on the 14th day and Unleavened Bread was on the 15th day. He could have so easily said that Firstfruits was on the 16th day if it was going to follow Unleavened Bread?

The Hebrew term for the Feast Day "sabbaths" is "Shabbaton." This term is used to describe a sabbath that occurs as a "Feast Day.' However, it observed similar to the prescribed weekly Sabbath or Shabbat. It is therefore clear that the "Feast of Firstfruits" occurs on the day after the weekly Sabbath or first day, (Sunday).

When you count 50 days to arrive at Shavuot (Feast of Weeks, Pentecost) you must begin count from Firstfruits, seven sabbaths which equal 49 days and the following day which occurs on the 1st day of the week (Sunday) is going to be Shavuot (Feast of Weeks, Pentecost) It is also called Pentecost which is a Greek term that means fiftieth.

Lev. 23:24 And this shall be a statute for ever unto you: that in the seventh month, on the tenth day of the month, ye shall afflict your souls, and do no work at all, whether it be one of your own country or a stranger that sojourneth among you: 30. For on that day shall the priest make an atonement for you, to cleanse you, that ye may be clean from all your sins before the LORD. 31. It shall be a sabbath of rest unto you, and ye shall afflict your souls, by a statute forever.

(שַׁבַּת שַׁבָּתוֹן הִיא לָכֶם וְעִנִּיתֶם אֶת־נַפְשֹׁתֵיכֶם חֻקַּת עוֹלָם:)

The scripture in Hebrew reads "Shabbat Shabbaton" or Sabbath a Sabbath of rest. The scripture is expressing the fact that you must rest on Yom Kippur just as you do on the weekly Sabbath. When the scripture refers to a "feast day Sabbath," it uses the term "Shabbaton."

While reading the Bible, many people are oblivious to the fact that the writers expressed themselves in the Hebrew language. The culture, practices, and customs stand in the background of the language. To appreciate the book, you must try to understand the culture. The Hebrew language uses expressions that are unique only to the Hebrew people or the given culture of that day.

English is a language and culture. We use idioms such as "giving an arm or leg" to mean that you have a strong desire to have the object or service in question. If someone comes from another country and they hear that phrase, they would not understand why you would chop off your arm or leg to get that object or service that you desire.

The same is right in the Hebrew/Eber language. We read in Genesis 1:14... lights in the firmament for signs and seasons. The transliteration of the word "moedim" was the word seasons. If you just read this in English, it implied that the lights in the heavens were for the seasons of the year. The term for the seasons of the year is the word "onah." The term "moedim" literally means "festivals, appointed times, feast days, etc." but it can also reference the seasons of the year as well. The literal context of the word is for festivals, feast days and appointed times. The English transliteration of the term moedim implies only the seasons of the year. We must, therefore, remember that understanding the Bible through the lens of the Hebrew/Eber language is extremely important. Most people have a superficial, perfunctory understanding of the Bible.

During the time of Moses immediately after the Children of Israel crossed the Red Sea as slaves and gathered on the other side free people. They rejoiced and sang a song regarding "the horse and the chariot He has cast into the sea." They traveled for three days without water and arrived at Marah, where the water was bitter. They began to grumble against Moses asking, "what are we to drink." Moses appealed to the Most High who led him to a certain piece of wood which he threw into the water and the water became fresh. He also led them to Elam where" *there were twelve springs of water and seventy palm trees and they camped near the water."* Ex. 15:27

On the 15th day of the second month, they came into the desert of Sin between Elim and Sinai. Once there, they began complaining again.

"Would that we had died at the Lord's hand in the land of Egypt, as we sat by the fleshpots and ate our fill of bread! However, you had to lead us into this desert to make the whole community die of famine!" Ex. 16:3

The Most High then rained down bread from heaven to feed the people. In the evening there were quail, and in the morning after the dew evaporated, there on the surface of the desert lay fine flakes like hoarfrost on the ground. (Manna is falling right now in some countries in Africa). It is incredible that most people in America don't know this.

After arriving at Rephidim, they complained again about the

lack of water. They began to ask Moses *"Why did you ever make us leave Egypt? Ex.17:3"* The Most High then commanded Moses to strike a rock and water came out of the rock. At Rephidim, they fought against Amalek and while Moses stood on the hill with Aaron and Hur, Joshua engaged Amalek in battle. Whenever Aaron and Hur got tired and allowed the hand of Moses to lower, Joshua began to lose. They finally supported Moses arms and Joshua defeated Amalek.

In the third month, they arrived at the wilderness of Sinai and camped at the foot of the mountain. Almost 47 days had passed since they had left Egypt. They were approaching the time of Shavuot which is fifty days after the Feast of Firstfruits.

Ex. 19:3 And Moses went up unto God, and the LORD called unto him out of the mountain, saying, Thus shalt thou say to the house of Jacob, and tell the children of Israel; 4. Ye have seen what I did unto the Egyptians, and how I bare you on eagles' wings and brought you unto myself. 5. Now, therefore, if ye will obey my voice indeed, and keep my covenant, then ye shall be a peculiar treasure unto me above all people: for all the earth is mine: 6. And ye shall be unto me a kingdom of priests and a holy nation. These are the words which thou shalt speak unto the children of Israel. 7. And Moses came and called for the elders of the people and laid before their faces all these words which the LORD commanded him. 8. And all the people answered together, and said, all that the LORD hath spoken we will do. And Moses returned the words of the people unto the LORD.

This period is also known as the Feast of Weeks. Lev.23:15-16 And ye shall count unto you from the morrow after the sabbath, from the day that ye brought the sheaf of the wave offering; seven sabbaths shall be complete: 16. Even unto the morrow after the seventh sabbath shall ye number fifty days;

and ye shall offer a new meat offering unto the LORD.

Counting was the anticipation of the event that was to take place. We should take notice that in Ex. 19, someone had been physically counting the days because they knew the exact day and time. (third month, 1st day). They were instructed by Moses to prepare to be ready against the third day which was going to be the fiftieth day. They got to the foot of the mountain on the 47th days and three more days would put them at the 50th day. This day was called Shavuot (day of Pentecost, Feast of Weeks). It comes from the word shavua which means week. The word "Shavuot" is the plural form of the word Shavua which means "weeks."

The period between Passover and Shavuot is the time of the counting of the omer. The "Omer" is a Hebrew word that means "sheaves of a harvested crop," and in ancient times the Hebrews brought the omer to the Temple as an offering. The count ends after 49 days and the following day is the fiftieth day called Shavuot. During this time Psalms, 119 is read in preparation for the 50th day and a time of reflection and remembrance of the journey from Egypt to Mt. Sinai.

"Lev. 23:15-16 And ye shall count unto you from the morrow after the sabbath, from the day that ye brought the sheaf of the wave offering; seven sabbaths shall be complete: 16. Even unto the morrow after the seventh sabbath shall ye number fifty days; and ye shall offer a new meat offering unto the LORD.

וּסְפַרְתֶּם□כֶם מִמָּחֳרַת הַשַּׁבָּת מִיּוֹם הֲבִיאֲכֶם אֶת־עֹמֶר הַתְּנוּפָה שֶׁבַע שַׁבָּתוֹת תְּמִימֹת)
:(תִּהְיֶינָה

Counting comes from the Hebrew/Eber word "cephar" which means to mark, tally, record, recount or celebrate. It has the same spelling as the Hebrew/Eber word "cephar" which means book. On this very day, the "Ten Utterances or Commandments, Book of the Law" was given to Moses and the children of Israel at the foot of Mt. Sinai. They marked or tallied the sheaves of the harvest until they received the "Book" or Ten Commandments.

We should also note that after Yahshua's resurrection, He made appearances during the time of the counting of the omer. On the 1st day of the omer, Yahshua appeared to Miriam and others. He also came among them after eight days and as recorded for 40 days.

John 20:1 The first day of the week cometh Mary Magdalene early, when it was yet dark, unto the sepulcher, and seeth the stone taken away from the tomb.

John 20:26 And after eight days again his disciples were within, and Thomas with them: then came Jesus, the doors being shut, and stood in the midst, and said, Peace be unto you.

The writer Luke also wrote about the appearance on the Road to Emmaus. He indicated that the two of the disciples were actually conversing with Him about all the things that had occurred. They were discussing how the women came to the tomb and the tomb was empty. Yahshua began to expound unto them the scriptures beginning with Moses. (I wonder why?) He broke bread with them and then as soon as they recognized who He was, He disappeared.

Luke 24:27 And beginning at Moses and all the prophets, he expounded unto them in all the scriptures the things concerning himself. 28. And they drew nigh unto the village, whither they went: and he made as though he would have gone further. 29. But they constrained him, saying, abide with us: for it is toward evening, and the day is far spent. And he went in to tarry with them. 30. And it came to pass, as he sat at meat with them, he took bread and blessed it, and brake, and gave to them. 31. And their eyes were opened, and they knew him, and he vanished out of their sight. 32. And they said one to another, did not our heart burn within us, while he talked with us by the way, and while he opened to us the scriptures?

When they arrived in Jerusalem, Yahshua appeared to them again. He stood among the disciples, showed them his hands and feet, spoke with them and even ate a piece of baked fish and a honeycomb. Then He opened their minds to understand the scriptures.

44. And he said unto them, these are the words which I spake unto you, while I was yet with you, that all things must be fulfilled, which were written in the law of Moses, and in the prophets, and in the psalms, concerning me. 45. Then opened he their understanding, that they might understand the scriptures,

He then instructed them to stay in the city of Jerusalem. They were to wait for the promise of power from on high. The writer Luke went on to say that Yahshua led them out of the city to Bethany, raised his hand to bless them and was taken up to heaven. Without a doubt, you can tell that the writer Luke counted the omer because he knew how many days Yahshua was here after the crucifixion. They say that Luke is the writer of the book of Luke because it bears his name. He is also the one who wrote the book of Acts. I can't confirm nor deny that he wrote it. However, when you read Acts 1, it reads like the continuation of the book of Luke. He begins the book of Acts by discussing the commandments that he gave to the disciples. These were not new commandments, remember in Luke 24:44 He discussed with the disciples about the fulfillment of those things written in the 'Law of Moses." He then goes on to indicate that Yahshua was with them forty days. Who was doing the counting and why were they counting? They were counting the omer as instructed and knew when Yahshua ascended because they were anticipating the Feast of Shavuot. They were also anxiously waiting for the promise to be endued with power from on high, most likely to occur on Shavuot.

Acts 1:2 Until the day in which he was taken up, after that he through the Holy Ghost had given commandments unto the apostles whom he had chosen: 3. To whom also he shewed himself alive after his passion by many infallible proofs, being seen of them forty days, and speaking of the things pertaining to the kingdom of God: 4. And, being assembled together with them, commanded them that they should not depart from Jerusalem, but wait for the promise of the Father, which, saith he, ye have heard of me. 5. For John truly baptized with water, but ye shall be baptized with the Holy Ghost not many days hence. 6. When they, therefore, were come together, they asked of him, saying, Lord, wilt thou at this time restore again the kingdom to Israel? 7. And he said unto them, it is not for you to know the times or the seasons, which the Father hath put in his own power. 8. But ye shall receive power, after that the Holy Ghost comes upon you: and ye shall be witnesses unto me both in Jerusalem, and in all Judaea, and in Samaria, and unto the uttermost part of the earth. 9. And when he had spoken these things, while they beheld, he was taken up; and a cloud received him out of their sight.

What was so special about Shavuot? How does Shavuot relate to the time of Moses and the time of Yahshua? First of all, when I was a Christian, I was not taught that the day of Pentecost and Shavuot was the same feast day. Many theologians teach that the day of Pentecost was a fulfillment of a promise of the Holy Ghost. I thought that this Day of Pentecost was some new event which we now acknowledge as the day that the Holy Spirit came within them in the upper room. I never associated the Day of Pentecost with any Biblical feast days. I did not know that this Feast Day existed prior to the event that occurred in the upper room.

The Greeks and the English did a masterful job of hiding this feast day (Shavuot) under the banner of Pentecost. The reason why the Greeks called it Pentecost is because the name (Pentecost) means fifty. Through careful study and exegesis of scripture, I discovered that the day of Pentecost had the original name of the Feast of Shavuot. It was the fourth feast day prescribed by the Most High. Today, they refer to Shavuot as the Feast of Weeks. (seven weeks and one day) The word Shavuot comes from the Hebrew/Eber word Shavua which means week. The suffix or ending to the word "Shavu ot" (ot) makes the word plural meaning weeks. They count seven weeks from the day of Firstfruits plus one day makes the fiftieth day called Shavuot. The root of the word is "Sheva" which means seven.

שבועות
SHAVUOT

You spell Shavuot with the Hebrew/Eber letters shin, bet, vav, ayin, vav, and tav. The first two letters shin and bet give us the understanding of the number seven which is the parent root of the word Sheva (week). The balance of the word (Shavuot) is numerically coded to equal the number fifty.

Vav	=	6
Ayin	=	16
Vav	=	6
Tav	=	22
Total	=	50

שבועות

There is also a hidden meaning with the placement of the ayin between the two vavs. The Hebrew/Eber letter vav in its pictograph form looks like a nail or hook. The simplified meaning of the letter (vav) is connected or join two or more into partnership. The letter ayin means keen perception, understanding, spiritual insight and seeing beyond the obvious. What do you see? Do you see things from a physical or spiritual perspective? Ayin stands for both the inner and physical eye with the former spiritual views open.

With the letter ayin placed between two vavs in the Hebrew/Eber word Shavuot, there is a hidden message. It is the connection between physical insight and spiritual insight. It is the connection of the Torah and the Ruach Ha Chodesh, and the Set-apart Spirit. The counting of the omer for 50 days has the same numerical value as the Hebrew/Eber letter Nun.

The pictograph of the nun is the sperm or seed which represent life. It is the 14th letter of the Hebrew/Eber alphabet, which corresponds to the 14th day of Abib or Passover. The letter nun also means salvation or deliverance. The movement of 50 days from Passover to Shavuot went from great physical pain in slavery to spiritual enlightenment with the giving of the Torah at Mt. Sinai. The Torah was gifted to humanity to teach the man to live in peace and harmony in the physical realm. The physical manifestation of peace and harmony eventually leads to the spiritual realm.

During the 50 days of counting the omer, they read Psalm 119. On the 14th day of counting the omer, they read Psalm 119: 105 entitled, "NUN. Thy word *is* a lamp unto my feet, and a light unto my path." This scripture explains how the Torah will assist you with your daily walk (unto my feet), but eventually, it will become your spiritual guide on your life's journey (light unto my path). The Hebrew letter nun means seed, son, offspring, and water. The shape of the nun is like a sperm. Psalm 119 can read that the son is the lamp unto my feet.

The final Hebrew/Eber letter in the word Shavuot is the letter Tav. The pictograph of this letter is the shape of a cross or cross sticks. The meaning of the letter Tav is mark, sign, seal, and covenant. The letter tav is the 22nd letter in the Hebrew/ Eber aleph-bet and has a numerical value of 400. Tav is the final stamp of what has been and a signal for renewal. During this season of Shavuot, we are being instructed to move from the physical mode of operation to the spiritual by agreeing to become sealed by the covenant. The covenant was made with Abraham and we inherited the promises because we are descendants of Abraham, Isaac, and Jacob.

Gen. 15:13 And he said unto Abram, know of a surety that thy seed shall be a stranger in a land that is not theirs, and shall serve them; and they shall afflict them four hundred years; 14. And also that nation, whom they shall serve, will I judge: and afterward shall they come out with great substance.

Acts: 7:6 And God spoke on this wise, that his seed should sojourn in a strange land; and that they should bring them into bondage and entreat them evil four hundred years. 7. And the nation to whom they shall be in bondage will I judge, said God: and after that shall they come forth, and serve me in this place.

Shavuot celebrates the start of the wheat harvest and the end of the barley harvest and marks the anniversary of the day the Most High gave the Torah to the people at Mount Sinai. Most Christians do not see the correlation between the Mt. Sinai experience and the Upper Room. These two events were not only mirrored images of each other, but they were the two events alluded to with the two letters vav encasing the letter ayin in the name Shavuot. All the things that occurred at Mt. Sinai occurred in the Upper Room.

All the People:
In Exodus 19:8 the term "all the people" (kal ha'am) was used to describe those that were present at the foot of the mountain. The people answered together and said, "all that has Yahweh spoke, we will do." This answer that the people gave sounded like a wedding vow! In the book of Acts 2:1 it says that they were "all with one accord." In Acts 1:15 it indicates that there were 120 people there. *Acts 1:15 And in those days Peter stood up in the midst of the disciples, and said, (the number of names together were about a hundred and twenty,).* It appears that there was a total of twelves disciples there. (Judas was replaced) If each disciple brought 10 people over the age of 13 which is the minimum quorum necessary to recite certain prayers and certain ceremonies, that would be considered a minyan.

A minyan symbolizes the minimum number that constitutes a Hebrew community…. A minyan also describes a group which regularly prays together, usually in a space other than a formal sanctuary.

(The Encyclopedia of Jewish Symbols, Ellen Frankel and Betsy Platkin Teutsch, 1992, pp 111.)

Therefore, if each disciple brought a minyan, the total there would equal 120 people or all that was required for a perfect prayer meeting. All the people (kal ha'am) were at Mt. Sinai and in the Upper Room. The people were instructed at Mt. Sinai to be ready against the third day. They arrived at the foot of the mountain on the 47th day. The 3rd day would be Shavuot for on this day, Yahweh was going to come down to the people on Mt. Sinai. (*Ex. 19:11*) Before he made his final ascension, Yahshua instructed the Disciples to tarry or wait for the promise. They arrived at the Upper Room in great anticipation. Acts 2:1 describes the culmination of their waiting by indicating that the day of Shavuot (Pentecost) has fully come.

Old Testament:
The people prepared themselves for the third day which was Shavuot the fiftieth. The event that was scheduled to happen occurred in the morning on the day of Shavuot. Moses began detailing the occurrence in the book of Exodus 19:16 "*And it came to pass on the third day in the morning, that there were thunders and flashes of lightning and a thick cloud upon the mount, and the voice of the trumpet exceeding loud; so that all the people that were in the camp trembled.*" If the event occurred during the time of Moses in the morning, then the pattern would be that it should happen in the morning after the ascension of Yahshua while the disciples were waiting for the promise of power.

New Testament:
The Book of Acts chapter 2 confirms what we suspected all along. It begins by saying when the day (daylight) of Pentecost (Shavuot) has fully come. In that part of the world, daylight began at 6:00 am. It was around that time while they were gathered that the event began to unfold. No matter how long they had been in the upper room, the events unfolded during the daylight hours. The 15th verse of the same chapter

the disciple Paul explicates the fact that they were not drunk as it appeared to others that were observing them. He used the fact that it was morning during his expostulation. Who gets drunk this early in the morning he says?

Act 2:15 For these are not drunken, as ye suppose, seeing it is but the third hour of the day. 16. But this is that which was spoken by the prophet Joel; 17. And it shall come to pass in the last days, saith God, I will pour out of my Spirit upon all flesh: and your sons and your daughters shall prophesy, and your young men shall see visions, and your old men shall dream dreams: 18. And on my servants and on my handmaidens I will pour out in those days of my Spirit; and they shall prophesy: 19. And I will shew wonders in heaven above, and signs in the earth beneath; blood, and fire, and vapor of smoke: 20. The sun shall be turned into darkness, and the moon into blood, before that great and notable day of the Lord come 21. And it shall come to pass, that whosoever shall call on the name of the Lord shall be saved.

Old Testament:
While the people were gathered at the foot of the mountain that morning there came thunders and flashes of lightning from heaven, and a thick cloud covered the mountain. What is thunder? Thunder is the sound caused by lightning. Depending on the distance and nature of the flash, thunder can range from a sharp, loud crack to a long, low rumble (brontide). The sudden increase in pressure and temperature from lightning produces rapid expansion of the air surrounding and within a bolt of lightning.

(Wikipedia https://en.wikipedia.org/wiki/Thunder)

When the sound of thunder occurs, it frightens the person and creates a shudder of surprise. They say that the lion's roar and suddenness will frighten its prey and cause the prey to stop as if paralyzed which allows the lion to attack. In many parts of

Africa, YHWH is known as the "God of Thunder and Lightning."

The New Testament:
Interestingly enough, the Most High uses strict accuracy and precision when he executed Shavuot at the time of the experience in the Upper Room. Luke, the writer of the book of Acts, describes this event as "a sound from heaven."

If you were to ask a third grader to give you the name of a sound from heaven, he or she would say, "thunder." While they were in the room, a sound came from heaven (the sound of thunder). No wonder the letter to the Colossians indicates that this mystery was hidden for ages and generations. The Bible is a set of writings (scriptures) that many refer to "old and new," but they all agree.

Colossian 1:16 Even the mystery which hath been hidden from ages and generations, but now is made manifest to his saints.

Old Testament:
While at the foot of the mountain, the people heard the sound of thunder and they also heard the voice of the Shofar (trumpet). The term used here "voice" is the Hebrew word qol. This word comes from an unused root meaning to call aloud, voice or proclamation. Whenever a loud call is made, it is meant to alarm, awaken and heighten your senses to an event that is about to occur.

The voice was that of the Shofar. During those times, they used the horns of an animal, usually the ram. They carved out the interior of the horn and blew air through it. The horn is usually narrow at one end and wider at the other end. The sound was used to awaken, alarm and gather the people together for an event. This sound of the shofar was unusual and had a similar effect on humans as does the sound of thunder. In ancient times at a King's coronation, the shofar would be blown. When the Hebrew people were about to engage in battle, they sounded the shofar. There were many uses for the shofar including sounding the shofar to alert people of the entrance of the Bridegroom at a wedding. This is the sound that they heard at the foot of the mountain.

New Testament:
While the 120 or minyan (10 men or women comprised a quorum for legal prayer group called a minyan) of each disciple was tarrying in the upper room, they heard the sound from heaven as of a mighty rushing wind. Interestingly enough, the horn, whether it is a saxophone, clarinet or trumpet, is considered to be a "wind" instrument. The breath or (Ruach) of a man is blown through this dead animal's horn in some cases to save the life of someone. Even today, we use the car horn to alert people of possible danger.

Therefore, the animal sacrificed part of his life to save the life of a human being. Sounds similar to Genesis chapter 3 when they heard the "voice" of the Most High walking in the cool of the day (morning) and called out to Adam. Adam and Eve were hiding because they had disobeyed the Most High and had taken fig leaves to hide their nakedness. The Most High skinned an innocent animal and made coverings for them. Man, always used animals as a sacrifice for the sins of man.

The sound of a mighty rushing wind (shofar) entered the room where they were sitting! The exact thing that happened at the foot of Mt. Sinai during the time of Moses.

Old Testament:
When all the people heard the noise coupled with the thick cloud that engulfed the mount, they trembled with fear. What an awesome event! The people began to shake and shudder

with terror and fear because of what they saw and heard.

New Testament:
While in the upper room the rushing "mighty" wind filled all the house where they were sitting. This powerful sound filled this small room, and the implication was that the people were suddenly and unexpectedly experiencing a feeling of awe and inspiration concerning this unusual occurrence. Yahshua told them in a prior dialogue that the "wind bloweth where it listeth" or appears whenever or wherever. No one knows where the wind came from or where it is going. You don't know when the wind becomes a tornado, nor can you prepare for it. The sound of the mighty rushing wind filled the whole house.

Old Testament:
Exodus 19:18, Says the Mount Sinai was entirely in smoke because Yahweh descended upon it in a fire. The Most High was in the fire. This spectacular event appears to be the culmination and re-visitation of the covenant with Abraham. When a deep sleep fell upon Abram and Yahweh told him that his seed would be strangers in a land that is not theirs and they will serve them four hundred years. A smoking oven and burning torch passed between the pieces of the animals that had been slain. (three-year-old female goat, a three-year-old ram, a turtledove, and a young pigeon) *Gen. 15:17*

The covenant of the Ten Commandments was being brought before the people by the element of fire. The people may not have known what was going on, but Moses was not unfamiliar with meeting Yahweh in a fire.

Ex. 3:2 And the angel of the LORD appeared unto him in a flame of fire out of the midst of a bush: and he looked, and, behold, the bush burned with fire, and the bush was not consumed. 3. And Moses said, I will now turn aside, and see this great sight, why the bush is not burnt. 4. And when the LORD saw that he turned aside to see, God called unto him out of the midst of the bush, and said, Moses, Moses. And he said, here am I. Yahweh called Moses from the midst of the bush that did not burn. From this meeting, Moses received his instruction and commission to lead the children of Israel out of bondage. The Most High moves in the midst of the fire. *Deut. 4:34 For the LORD thy God is a consuming fire, even a jealous God. Heb. 12:39 For our God is a consuming fire.*

New Testament:
After the sound entered the room and filled all the house, there appeared cloven (divided) tongues as of fire, and it set upon each one of them. (Acts 2:8) We see a quite striking parallel between what happened at the foot of the mountain and what took place in the upper room. The fire that appeared at Mt. Sinai was also in the upper chamber.

The Feast Day events are consistent, both in the Old Testament (Torah) and the New Testament (Brit Hadashah). It is complicated to understand the upper room event without knowing the Feast of Shavuot. The problem is that we read the Bible in the English transliteration about the Day of Pentecost as if this event was an independent happening and perhaps was not Hebraically related. The Day of Pentecost is the Feast Day that all Hebrews keep, and its original name is Shavuot.

We should be reminded that John the baptizer explained to the disciples, that when the Holy Spirit appears it would bring fire. *Luke 3:16 John answered, saying unto them all, I indeed baptize you with water; but one mightier than I cometh, the latchet of whose shoes I am not worthy to unloose: he shall baptize you with the Holy Ghost and with fire:*

Old Testament:
As the voice (qal) of the shofar became louder and louder, Moses spoke, and Elohim answered him by voice. *Ex. 19:19* After the fire came, Moses spoke. When you are in the presence of Yahweh, and the anointing comes over you, you will speak. Jeremiah refers to it as a fire shut up in his bones. *Jer. 20:9*

New Testament:
After the tongues of fire sat upon each of them, they (the people with the tongues of fire) began to speak in other tongues as the spirit gave utterance. *Acts 2:4* There is considerable controversy over whether speaking in tongues is real, fake or demonic. I have spoken in tongues and know that it is life changing.

No one coached me on how to receive the Holy Spirit nor was I ever informed of the history or its Biblical precedence. My approach to religion was merely academic. When I received the Holy Spirit (Ruach HaChodesh), it was an excellent experience. I received the Holy Spirit in the privacy of my home. I had the experience of speaking in another tongue that I had not learned in school or anywhere. My life changed after that experience.

The Ten Commandments:
Elohim began to speak all the words of the Ten Commandments (ten utterances) unto the people. The first one was not to have any other Elohim before Him. We are not to make images of anything in heaven or earth and bow down to them. He let them know not to use his Name in vain. He said to remember (Zakar) the Sabbath day and keep (Shamar-guard) it holy (Chodesh-separate from all other days. He spoke other six commands and went back up into the mountain. While in the mountain the Most High gave Moses instructions on how to build the tabernacle, make the furniture and the clothing

for the priesthood. But when the people saw that Moses did not come down from the mountain, they suspected that He had disappeared. They then brought their concerns to Aaron. They broke off earrings and other gold items and made a golden calf and proclaimed their own Feast Day unto Yahweh. The Most High instructed Moses to get down from the mountain and check on the people.

They corrupted themselves immediately after they received the Ten Commandments. They made an image and bowed down to it. The anger of Elohim kindled against the people to the extent that Moses had to plead to that Yahweh grant them mercy and not wipe them off the face of the earth. Moses reminded Elohim about the covenant that He made with Abraham, Isaac, and Jacob that his seed would be like the stars of heaven and that they (seed) would inherit the land forever.

Yahweh sent Moses back down from the mountain with two stone tablets engraved by the hand of the Most High. What Moses found when he returned made him so angry that he took the tablets and broke them at the foot of the mountain. He saw them worshiping the golden calf. He took the calf which they had made, burned it in the fire, and ground it to powder and made them drink it. Then Moses made them make a choice and asked to decide who was on Yahweh's side and let him come. Then he gathered together the sons of Levi and instructed them to get their sword and go throughout the gates and slay every man and his brother, companion, and neighbor. The children of Israel did what Moses instructed and there fell of the people that day about three thousand men.

Ex. 32:26 Then Moses stood in the gate of the camp, and said, who is on the LORD'S side? Let him come unto me. And all the sons of Levi gathered themselves together unto him. 27. And he said unto them, thus saith the LORD God of Israel, put every man his sword by his side, and go in and out from gate to gate throughout the camp, and slay every man his brother, and every man his companion, and every man his neighbor. 28. And the children of Levi did according to the word of Moses: and there fell of the people that day about three thousand men.

The Most High wiped out about 3000 people that day. He wiped out about 3000 people but spared the others. It is apparent that Yah extended His mercy that day. What I found striking was that the same thing in reverse happened in the book of Acts.

Acts 2:38 Then Peter said unto them, Repent, and be baptized every one of you in the name of Jesus Christ for the remission of sins, and ye shall receive the gift of the Holy Ghost. 39. For the promise is unto you, and to your children, and to all that are afar off, even as many as the Lord our God shall call. 40. And with many other words did he testify and exhort, saying, Save yourselves from this untoward generation. 41. Then they that gladly received his word were baptized: and the same day there were added unto them about three thousand souls.

Israel never lost a soul because those 3000 that perished at the time of Moses, were restored after the Upper Room experience.

Feast of Shavuot

Old Testament	New Testament
Exodus 19:11 All the people	Acts 2:1 All with one accord
Exodus 19:16 The third day	Acts 2:1 Day of Pentecost

Old Testament	New Testament
Exodus 19:16 In the morning	Acts 2:15 Third hour
Exodus 19:16 Thunderings	Acts 2:2 Sound from heaven
Exodus 19:16 Trumpet	Acts 2:2 Rushing mighty wind
Exodus 19:16 All…trembled	Acts 2:2 Filled the house
Exodus 19:18 Fire	Acts 2:3 Tongues of fire
Exodus 19:18 Moses spoke	Acts 2:4 Began to speak
Exodus 19:19 God's voice	Acts 2:4 Spirit gave utterance
Exodus 19:25 Speak	Acts 2:14 Peter said to the people
Exodus 32:28 About 3000	Acts 2:41 About 3000

Chapter Fifteen: The Ten Commandments

I participated in a Christian church for many years in various capacities including ministry for about eighteen years of my life. That period lasted nearly two decades. We never celebrated the Feast of Shavuot or what we called the Day of Pentecost. I wonder why?

I'm not sure why it was not considered a holiday, because most sermons that we heard during my tenure in Christianity included quotes from Acts 2:1-8 and Acts 2:38. Those are scriptures that reference the receiving what we called the Holy Ghost. To me, it seems odd that we never declared the Day of Pentecost a holiday.

During the time that the Children of Israel were initially wandering in the wilderness, at the end of fifty days, the Most High gifted them the Ten Commandments. The experience was similar to the observance of a marriage ceremony. The people were instructed to prepare for the third day and were brought to the foot of the mountain to receive their contract (Ten Instructions). In the typical Hebrew wedding, the bridegroom provides the bride a (ketubah/marriage contract), and the bride must agree to the terms of the agreement.

In the ceremony of today, the performer of the wedding asks them both if they will agree to love, cherish and care for one another, whether rich or poor, in sickness and in health, forsaking all others, till death they do part, and they individually say the words, I do. At the foot of the mountain, our forefathers said, "all that you say we will do." We agreed to the terms our marriage contract with the Most High at Mt. Sinai. At the end of fifty days, the Most High gave the Ten Commandments or Ten Utterances. We were betrothed to the

Most High like a bride.

One of the names of the Ten Commandments is the Torah. When the Greeks transliterated the scriptures, they renamed the Torah to the word "nomos" or law. This term law has created much controversy in Christianity.

Most ministers preach that Yahshua abolished the Torah/ Law. The reason behind this teaching was to get everyone to reject the Ten Commandments or Torah. If you follow their logic, it is lawful to murder. They are also saying that it is permitted to commit adultery and steal. They are also saying that you can have other names beside Yahweh even though He warned that He is a jealous Elohim.

The Bible does not support this kind of nonsense! There is a sinister motive behind the rejection of the Torah (law). The main reason why the Catholic Church promoted this doctrine was to reject the Sabbath. If they can get you to defile the Sabbath, the violation of the other commandments would naturally follow.

Constantine the self-proclaimed Pontifex Maximus declared that he had supreme authority on the earth and that he was the replacement for Christ. He commanded everyone under his power in the empire, to worship on the venerable day of the sun or the first day of the week, and they still comply today. The churches of today are in sync with Constantine's authority. They are obedient like a child is to his parents.

Preachers recite quotes from Yahshua as if they supersede the Torah when in fact, Yahshua quoted the Torah. Why would he go against his word? He cited the Torah 26 times and the entire Tanakh (Old Testament) 78 times.

How is it that we can read things in the New Testament and not know that it was written in the Torah long before, but we reject the Old Testament (Torah). Yahshua told the people several times to keep His commandments.

Mat. 5:19 Whosoever, therefore, shall break one of these least commandments, and shall teach men so, he shall be called the least in the kingdom of heaven: but whosoever shall do and teach them, the same shall be called great in the kingdom of heaven.

Mat. 19:17 And he said unto him, why callest thou me good? there is none good but one, that is, God: but if thou wilt enters into life, keep the commandments.

Note the Torah (Ex. 20:6 And shewing mercy unto thousands of them that love me and keep my commandments."

John 14:15 If you love me keep my commandments.

Mat. 22:36 Master, which is the great commandment in the law? 37. Jesus said unto him, thou shalt love the Lord thy God with all thy heart, and with all thy soul, and with all thy mind. 38. This is the first and great commandment.

Note the Torah (Deut. 6:5 And thou shalt love the LORD thy God with all thine heart, and with all thy soul, and with all thy might.)

39. And the second is like, unto it, thou shalt love thy neighbor as thyself. 40. On these two commandments hang all the law and the prophets.

Note the Torah (Lev. 19:18 Thou shalt not avenge, nor bear any grudge against the children of thy people, but thou shalt love thy neighbor as thyself: I *am* the LORD.)

Mark 12:28 And one of the scribes came and having heard them reasoning together, and perceiving that he had answered them well, asked him, which is the first commandment of all? 29. And Jesus answered him, the first of all the commandments is, Hear, O Israel; The Lord our God is one Lord: 30. And thou shalt love the Lord thy God with all thy heart, and with all thy soul, and with all thy mind, and with all thy strength: this is the first commandment.

Note the Torah (Deut. 6:4 Hear, O Israel: The LORD our God *is* one LORD: 5. And thou shalt love the LORD thy God with all thine heart, and with all thy soul, and with all thy might.)

Note the Torah (Ex. 20:6 And shewing mercy unto thousands of them that love me and keep my commandments.)

John 15:10 If ye keep my commandments, ye shall abide in my love; even as I have kept my Father's commandments and abide in his love.

Note the Torah (Ex. 20:6 And shewing mercy unto thousands of them that love me and keep my commandments.)

Knowing that Yahshua was quoting the Torah lets us know that He would not go against His word.

John 5:39 Search the scriptures; for in them ye think ye have eternal life: and they are they which testify of me.

At the time that Yahshua quoted those words, there was no New Testament at all. Most scholars believe that Matthew wrote his book between AD 80-90. Mark wrote his book between AD 50 – 60. The text of Luke was the second Gospel written after the book of Mark (AD 70) because he used Mark as his sources. John wrote his book between AD 85 – 95. The first book in the New Testament (Brit Hadashah) was written almost 20 years after the death of Yahshua. When Yahshua spoke those words, He was quoting the Torah because He was the Torah incarnate. The Ten Commandments were given at Mt. Sinai, and each time He cited them, He took us back to the Feast of Shavuot (Day of Pentecost).

The Ten Commandments were not a set of laws; they were instructions on how to live.

The first four of the Ten Commandments contain our duty to Elohim (God), and the other six contain our responsibility to our fellow man.

These instructions if appropriately followed will create a harmonious society where people honor and respect one another. In this society called America, stealing, killing and adultery are so common that we have become immune to its effect on our psyche. We have developed a sort of scar tissue on our brain and hearts relative to sins (violation of Torah) that we see and commit daily.

Elohim (God) had every intention of revealing His Torah at the time of Shavuot (Pentecost). When Elohim (God) spoke His promises to Abraham, long before Moses the book of Torah, he spoke these words.

Gen. 26:4 And I will make thy seed to multiply as the stars of heaven and will give unto thy seed all these countries, and in thy seed shall all the nations of the earth be blessed; 5. Because that Abraham obeyed my voice and kept my charge, my commandments, my statutes, and my laws. עֵקֶב אֲשֶׁר־שָׁמַע אַבְרָהָם בְּקֹ֑לִי וַיִּשְׁמֹר מִשְׁמַרְתִּי מִצְוֹתַי חֻקּוֹתַי וְתוֹרֹתָי:

The term that was used for "laws" was Toroti which was the plural form or Torah and the "I" sound at the end represents personal possessive which is why they placed the word "my' in front of it. The transliteration of the Bible made the term Torah as law. The Torah is more than a legal name. The word Torah as used in the book of Genesis long before the Ten Commandments.

The simple meaning of the word Torah comes from the word "yarah" which means to shoot out the hand as pointing. It also means to show, indicate, to teach, instruct, to lay a foundation, to sprinkle, to water, to shoot like an arrow. The Hebrew/Eber word yarah begins with the letter yod which means hand. The hands on the body are critical as we use them to work, build and provide for our families. The Torah comes from a verb which has to do with instruction.

Instruction from a parent to a child (Prov. 1:8, 3:1, 4:2, 7:2)
Doctrine for instruction via the Prophets (Isa. 1:10, 8:16, 42:4, 21)
Legal instruction as in the "law of sacrifice" (Lev. 6:7, 7:7)
    Mosaic Revelation (Josh. 1:8)

The Torah involves faith, action, and obedience. Elohim (God) gave the Torah on the fiftieth day at the foot of the mountain. In the book of Genesis, the word Torah is also spelled out using a system of counting in Hebrew, every 50 letters.

The first word of the Bible (B'reshit) has the first letter of the word (Torah in the last letter of B'reshit). בְּרֵאשִׁית

Fifty letters later, we find the second letter of the word Torah in the letter "vav" where we get the sound of "o." The word used is the Hebrew/Eber word (tehom), which means the deep. Gen. 1:2 תְּהוֹם

Fifty letters later, the Hebrew/Eber letter "resh" where we get the sound of "r." It appears in the word (viyiera) meaning "and He saw." Gen. 1:4. וַיַּרְא

Fifty letters later, the Hebrew/Eber letter "hey" where we get the sound "h." It appears in the word (Elohim) which means God. Gen. 1:5
אֱלֹהִים

The Tav, vav, resh and hey spell out the word Torah counting every 50 letters. You get a better understanding of Shavuot when you use the Hebrew language. From the beginning, Elohim (God) had intentions on giving the Torah and the Holy Spirit on the 50th day called Shavuot (Day of Pentecost).

The Ten Commandments:
Exodus 20:1 And God spoke all these words, saying,
1. I *am* the LORD thy God, which have brought thee out of the land of Egypt, out of the house of bondage. Love and Honor His name YHWH. There was no other Elohim that had the power to bring us out of the land of Egypt. He put the Egyptian gods to shame during the time of the ten plagues.

2. Thou shalt have no other gods before me. Thou shalt not make unto thee any graven image or any likeness *of anything* that *is* in heaven above, or that *is* in the earth beneath, or that *is* in the water under the earth: thou shalt not bow down thyself to them, nor serve them: for I the LORD thy God *am* a jealous God, visiting the iniquity of the fathers upon the children unto the third and fourth *generation* of them that hate me; And shewing mercy unto thousands of them that love me and keep my commandments.

You are the "bride" of the Most High. He wants your complete devotion, and anything less is similar to a spouse who is cheating on her mate. If we found our spouse to be unfaithful, most likely we would head for an attorney to file for a divorce because we don't exercise the ability to forgive but we want the Most High to forgive us.

3. Thou shalt not take the name of the LORD thy God in vain; for the LORD will not hold him guiltless that taketh his name in vain. Revere the name! His very character and story exist within His name. Do not use His name in common ways. If you disrespect His name, you will suffer severe consequences. We should spread His name throughout the world.

4. Remember the sabbath day, to keep it holy. Six days shalt thou labor, and do all thy work: But the seventh day *is* the sabbath of the LORD thy God: *in it* thou shalt not do any work, thou, nor thy son, nor thy daughter, thy manservant, nor thy maidservant, nor thy cattle, nor thy stranger that *is* within thy gates; For *in* six days the LORD made heaven and earth, the sea, and all that in them *is,* and rested the seventh day: wherefore the LORD blessed the sabbath day and hallowed it.

Remember (Zakar) the Sabbath, (Shamar) guard it like a warrior would guard something precious. He puts his life on the line to protect it. Shabbat, (Sabbath) should be set apart from the rest of the week and all problems should be put away. Shabbat mirrors the seven days of creation.

5.Honor thy father and thy mother: that thy days may be long upon the land which the LORD thy God giveth thee. Honor and cherish the authority of your parents that you may have a long life. This commandment comes with a promise. The commandment has a promise of long life should you respect and honor your parents.

6. Thou shalt not kill. Love your neighbor by honoring his life

and the life of others. You can also murder with your tongue with cruel words that hurt others.

7. Thou shalt not commit adultery. Love your neighbor by honoring his wife or husband. The term adultery is closely related to the word idolatry which is the worship of other gods. When we worship things, we become like a cheating spouse.

8. Thou shalt not steal. Respect your neighbor's property as if it was your own. The lesson is that you need to have your own things because you will value them because you worked hard for them. It hurts for someone to take what you worked so hard for. This act is an imitation of Ha Satan. He comes to steal, kill and destroy.

9. Thou shalt not bear false witness against thy neighbor. Respect your neighbor's reputation and don't lie on him. All liars will share hell with Ha Satan. No one trusts a liar.

10. Thou shalt not covet thy neighbor's house, thou shalt not covet thy neighbor's wife, nor his manservant, nor his maidservant, nor his ox, nor his ass, nor anything that *is* thy neighbor's.

 Love your neighbor by honoring all that he has from your heart. To show honor to your neighbor means you are happy for him that the Most High has provided for him. Just as the Most High has supplied for your neighbor, He will do the same for you and even more. Don't go after your neighbor's things.

The Ten Commandments:
It is apparent that the Most High wanted us to commit acts that will help us live in harmony with Him and our fellow

man. Each action had a reward and a consequence. If we adhered to these ten commands, our lives would be more peaceful and complete. These are the principles of life that have withstood the test of time for thousands of years.

It is time that we take a closer look at the feast days. Now we know that they are not mere words in a book. They all related to Yahshua in some form or fashion. Unfortunately, the Christian world does not see it like that. They continue to practice paganism and tradition. We pray that we have somehow shed some light on the Feast Days of YHWH and many who read this book will begin to observe them. Shalom talmideem thank you for letting me share with you!

Bible Translation:

Name	Pictograph	Meaning	Name	Pictograph	Meaning
Aleph		Ox / strength / leader	Lamed		Staff / goad / control / "toward"
Bet		House / "in"	Mem		Water / chaos
Gimmel		Foot / camel / pride	Nun		Seed / fish / activity / life
Dalet		Tent door / pathway	Samekh		Hand on staff / support / prop
Hey		Lo! Behold! "The"	Ayin		Eye / to see / experience
Vav		Nail / peg / add / "And"	Pey		Mouth / word / speak
Zayin		Plow / weapon / cut off	Tsade		Man on side / desire / need
Chet		Tent wall / fence / separation	Qof		Sun on horizon / behind
Tet		Basket / snake / surround	Resh		Head / person / first
Yod		Arm and hand / work / deed	Shin		Eat / consume / destroy
Kaf		Palm of hand / to open	Tav		Mark / sign / covenant

Now all these things happened unto them for ensamples: and they are written for our admonition, upon whom the ends of the world have come. 1Cor. 10:11

Bible Translation dates:

A.D. 600 - The Roman Catholic Church declares Latin as the only language for Scripture.

A.D. 680 - Caedmon, English poet and monk, renders Bible books and stories into Anglo Saxon poetry and song.

A.D. 735 - Bede, English historian, and monk translate the Gospels into Anglo Saxon.

A.D. 775 - The Book of Kells, a richly decorated manuscript containing the Gospels and other writings, is completed by Celtic monks in Ireland.

Circa A.D. 865 - Saints Cyril and Methodius begin translating the Bible into Old Church Slavonic.

A.D. 950 - The Lindisfarne Gospels manuscript is translated into Old English.

Circa A.D. 995-1010 - Aelfric, an English abbot, translates parts of Scripture into Old English.

A.D. 1205 - Stephen Langton, theology professor and later Archbishop of Canterbury, creates the first chapter divisions in the books of the Bible.

A.D. 1229 - Council of Toulouse strictly forbids and prohibits lay people from owning a Bible.

A.D. 1325 - English hermit and poet, Richard Rolle de Hampole, and English poet William Shoreham translate the Psalms into metrical verse.

Circa A.D. 1330 - Rabbi Solomon ben Ismael first places chapter divisions in the margins of the Hebrew Bible.

A.D. 1381-1382 - John Wycliffe and associates, in defiance of the organized Church, believing that people should be permitted to read the Bible in their own language, begin to translate and produce the first handwritten manuscripts of the entire Bible in English. These include the 39 Old Testament books, 27 New Testament books, and 14 Apocrypha books.

A.D. 1388 - John Purvey revises Wycliffe's Bible.

A.D. 1415 - 31 years after Wycliffe's death, the Council of Constance charges him with more than 260 counts of heresy.

A.D. 1428 - 44 years after Wycliffe's death, church officials dig up his bones, burn them, and scatter the ashes on Swift River.

A.D. 1455 - After the invention of the printing press in Germany, Johannes Gutenberg produces the first printed Bible, the Gutenberg Bible, in the Latin Vulgate.

A.D. 1516 - Desiderius Erasmus produces a Greek New Testament, the forerunner to the Textus Receptus.

A.D. 1517 - Daniel Bomberg's Rabbinic Bible contains the first printed Hebrew version (Masoretic text) with chapter divisions.

A.D. 1522 - Martin Luther translates and publishes the New Testament for the first time into German from the 1516 Erasmus version.

A.D. 1524 - Bamberg prints a second edition Masoretic text prepared by Jacob ben Chayim.

A.D. 1527 - Erasmus publishes a fourth edition Greek-Latin translation.

A.D. 1530 - Jacques Lefèvre d'Étaples completes the first French language translation of the entire Bible.

A.D. 1535 - Myles Coverdale's Bible completes Tyndale's work, producing the first complete printed Bible in the English language. It includes the 39 Old Testament books, 27 New Testament books, and 14 Apocrypha books.

A.D. 1536 - Martin Luther translates the Old Testament into the commonly-spoken dialect of the German people, completing his translation of the entire Bible in German.

A.D. 1536 - Tyndale is condemned as a heretic, strangled, and burned at the stake.

A.D. 1537 - The Matthew Bible (commonly known as the Matthew-Tyndale Bible), a second complete printed English translation, is published, combining the works of Tyndale, Coverdale and John Rogers.

A.D. 1539 - The Great Bible, the first English Bible authorized for public use, is printed.

A.D. 1546 - Roman Catholic Council of Trent declares the Vulgate as the exclusive Latin authority for the Bible.

A.D. 1553 - Robert Estienne publishes a French Bible with chapter and verse divisions. This system of numbering becomes widely accepted and is still found in most Bible's today.

A.D. 1560 - The Geneva Bible is printed in Geneva, Switzerland. It is translated by English refugees and published by John Calvin's brother-in-law, William Whittingham. The Geneva Bible is the first English Bible to add numbered verses to the chapters. It becomes the Bible of the Protestant Reformation, more popular than the 1611 King James Version for decades after its original release.

A.D. 1568 - The Bishop's Bible, a revision of the Great Bible, is introduced in England to compete with the popular but "inflammatory toward the institutional Church" Geneva Bible.

A.D. 1582 - Dropping its 1,000-year-old Latin only policy, the Church of Rome produces the first English Catholic Bible, the Rheims New Testament, from the Latin Vulgate.

A.D. 1592 - The Clementine Vulgate (authorized by Pope Clementine VIII), a revised version of the Latin Vulgate, becomes the authoritative Bible of the Catholic Church.

A.D. 1609 - The Douay Old Testament is translated into English by the Church of Rome, to complete the combined Douay-Rheims Version.

A.D. 1611 - The King James Version, also called the "Authorized Version" of the Bible is published. It is said to be the most printed book in the history of the world, with more than one billion copies in print.

A.D. 1663 - John Eliot's Algonquin Bible is the first Bible printed in America, not in English, but in the native Algonquin Indian language.

A.D. 1782 - Robert Aitken's Bible is the first English language (KJV) Bible printed in America.

A.D. 1790 - Matthew Carey publishes a Roman Catholic Douay-Rheims Version English Bible in America.

A.D. 1790 - William Young prints the first pocket-sized "school edition" King James Version Bible in America.

A.D. 1791 - The Isaac Collins Bible, the first family Bible (KJV), is printed in America.

A.D. 1791 - Isaiah Thomas prints the first illustrated Bible (KJV) in America.

A.D. 1808 - Jane Aitken (daughter of Robert Aitken), is the first woman to print a Bible.

A.D. 1833 - Noah Webster, after publishing his famous dictionary, releases his own revised edition of the King James Bible.

A.D. 1841 - The English Hexapla New Testament, a comparison of the original Greek language and six important English translations, is produced.

A.D. 1844 - The Codex Sinaiticus, a handwritten Koine Greek manuscript of both Old and New Testament texts dating back to the fourth century, is rediscovered by German Bible scholar Konstantin Von Tischendorf in the Monastery of Saint Catherine on Mount Sinai.

A.D. 1881-1885 - The King James Bible is revised and published as the Revised Version (RV) in England.

A.D. 1901 - The American Standard Version, the first major American revision of the King James Version, is published.

A.D. 1946-1952 - The Revised Standard Version is published.

A.D. 1947-1956 - The Dead Sea Scrolls are discovered.

A.D. 1971 - The New American Standard Bible (NASB) is published.

A.D. 1973 - The New International Version (NIV) is published.

A.D. 1982 - The New King James Version (NKJV) is published.

A.D. 1986 - The discovery of the Silver Scrolls, believed to be the oldest Bible text ever, is announced. They were found three years earlier in the Old City of Jerusalem by Gabriel Barkay of Tel Aviv University.

A.D. 1996 - The New Living Translation (NLT) is published.

A.D. 2001 - The English Standard Version (ESV) is published.

(Sources: Willmington's Bible handbook; www.greatsite.com; Crossway; Bible Museum; Biblica; Christianity Today; and Theopedia.)